Textured Embroidery

MILNER CRAFT SERIES

Textured Embroidery

JENNY BRADFORD

SALLY MILNER PUBLISHING

First published in 1993 by
Sally Milner Publishing Pty Ltd
558 Darling Street
Rozelle NSW 2039 Australia

Reprinted 1993

© Jenny and Don Bradford, 1993

Design by Gatya Kelly, Doric Order
Photography by Andre Martin
Diagrams by Don Bradford
Colour separation in Australia by CS Graphic Reproduction
Typeset in Australia by Asset Typesetting Pty Ltd
Printed in Australia by Impact Printing, Melbourne

National Library of Australia
Cataloguing-in-Publication data:

Bradford, Jenny, 1936-
    Textured embroidery.

    ISBN 1 86351 076 1.

    1.Embroidery — Patterns. I. Title. (Series : Milner craft series)

746.44041

ACKNOWLEDGEMENTS

I would like to thank all those who have helped me during the production of this my ninth book.

To my husband, Don, without whose help I would not even be tempted to start. He does all the things I am no good at; drawing wonderful diagrams, tipyng adn poofraedign (not to mention the washing and ironing).

To Helen Janocha of East Maitland, NSW, for designing a beautiful sweater based on lovely ideas for wool embroidery that she teaches. Helen can be contacted on telephone (049) 33 1219. To Pat Kane for her cute punchneedle teddy bear. To Joyce McKee of Toowoomba, Queensland, for her lovely interpretation in needle painting of an Australian bush scene.

To the following people for their interest, support and practical help in supplying materials for working the samples: Neree Hartog of DMC Needlecraft Pty. Ltd., Marrickville, NSW; Elizabeth White of DownUnder Designs, Seaforth, NSW (02) 948 5575. Cherie Shepherd of Victoria House Needlecraft, Mittagong, NSW (048) 71 1682, for Paternayan Persian Yarn; Kreinik Mfg. Co. Inc. of the USA for metallic and filament threads; Jennifer Newman, Minnamurra Threads, Glebe, NSW (02) 692 9582; Mary Hart-Davies, Kacoonda Enterprises, Somers, Victoria and Pioneer Craft of Sydney (02) 477 1239, for supply of template plastic used in the boxes.

My thanks also to Marylyn Verstraeten (03) 822 3137, artist in gold and silver, for allowing me to use an example of her work to embellish my embroidery.

I count myself very lucky to be able to entrust my work to Sally Milner and her team. My grateful thanks to them all, including Andre Martin, photographer, for the patience, understanding and talent they use to enhance my work.

LIST OF DIAGRAMS

CHAPTER FOUR

Flower and leaf symbols as listed at the beginning of the chapter.

CHAPTER FIVE

CONTENTS

DEDICATION

To all the needlewomen who touch my life with words of encouragement and thanks.

INTRODUCTION

Textured Embroidery is a title that could apply to a vast range of embroidery techniques too numerous to be covered in a single volume such as this. The work selected for this book fits into three main categories: floral work (that many readers will identify with Brazilian embroidery), wool embroidery and needle painting.

As with my other publications, careful attention has been given to providing clear instructions for all techniques used and projects detailed. Particular care has been given to the selection of threads for the embroidery, concentrating on those that are readily available, such as stranded cotton, Coton Perle and wool.

Those who are familiar with my book *Bullion Stitch Embroidery* will find the completely new range of stitches and flowers contained in this book can be used hand-in-hand with bullion stitch embroidery.

CHAPTER 1

MATERIALS

THREADS

All the flowers depicted in the sampler on the colour pages can be worked in a variety of threads depending on the type of work being done, the look you wish to achieve and the size of the design required.

The roses shown in section 1A on the sampler are an excellent example of the variety that can be achieved by varying the choice of threads. Coton Perle No. 8 has been used for the flower on the top line, the three roses on the second row are worked in wool (single strand of Paternayan), DMC Flower thread and Isafil machine embroidery thread respectively.

Note that wool threads and stranded cotton have a dull finish compared with the Coton Perle, silk or rayon threads. Further variation in size from that shown in the sampler can be achieved by the thickness of the wool chosen and the number of strands used when working with stranded cotton.

The following list of threads is intended as a guide for the beginner but all the stitches chosen for the flowers depicted will work well with almost any of the enormous variety of threads now available on the market. Some, such as shiny rayon threads will be more difficult to handle than those with which I have chosen to work. It is important to use threads that you enjoy working with and also to remember that varying the threads used in a design can add interest, texture and contrast.

STRANDED COTTON

There are several different brands available in this most commonly used embroidery thread. I personally prefer DMC as it is readily available in a superb range of colours and is of excellent quality.

Reference is made throughout the book to a range of stranded hand-dyed variegated threads marketed under the name of Minnamurra Threads. Hand dyed in Australia, they are a small range of beautifully coloured threads using DMC stranded cotton for the base. There are many other over-dyed and variegated stranded threads now available from specialty embroidery shops, most of them coming from the USA.

PEARL COTTON

Available in four different thicknesses, No. 3 (thickest), No. 5, No. 8 and No. 12. This is a shiny cotton thread that does not feature as much as I feel it should in embroidery in general. The main brand available is the DMC Coton Perle, with an excellent colour range in plain and variegated thread. Minnamurra Threads have a similar colour range available in Coton Perle No. 8 as in stranded cotton.

Over-dyed Coton Perle in No. 3, 5, 8 and 12, from the USA, is also available in some specialty shops.

FLOWER THREAD

This is a lovely, smooth 2 ply fine cotton thread with a firm twist by DMC, available in a good range of colours, most of them numbered in line with the stranded cotton shades.

WOOLS

There are many wools on the market providing a wide choice of thickness and colour. Do not ignore the fact that knitting wools can be used. These may stand up to repeated washing more successfully than tapestry wools, which are primarily designed for canvas work and not washable clothing.

DMC MEDICI

A very fine, smooth 2 ply wool excellent for very fine delicate work. A number of strands may be used together.

APPLETONS CREWEL WOOL

A fine 2 ply wool in a beautiful range of colours. Slightly fluffier than Medici. A number of strands may be used together.

PATERNAYAN PERSIAN YARN

A 3 ply stranded tapestry wool in an excellent colour range. A single strand is approximately equivalent to a 3 ply knitting yarn.

TAPESTRY WOOLS

Available in a wide range of colours. A firm 4 ply twist, approximately equivalent to 8 ply knitting wool. DMC and Appletons both have excellent colour ranges.

KNITTING WOOLS

Rowan 4 ply 'Botany' and 8 ply double knitting wools are those used by Kaffe Fassett for his beautiful knitting and tapestry designs. These are available in a lovely range of shaded colours not always obtainable in the more commonly used brands of knitting wools.

Specialty wool shops dealing in more exotic knitting yarns can be inspirational. The hearts on the cream blanket on the colour pages are outlined with a silk and viscose knitting yarn purchased from one such shop.

HAND-DYED WOOLS

Many hand-dyed variegated wools are now available. Those used in this book are by Mary Hart-Davies who dyes a range of wool threads in various weights and twists that are marketed under the trade name of Kacoonda. Hand-dyed wools are often available from spinners' and weavers' groups or from shops specialising in fibre arts. There are also ranges of over-dyed wools, equivalent in weight to Appletons 'Crewel' or DMC 'Medici', available from some specialty shops.

SILK THREADS

There are many silk threads currently available that can be used for the embroidery in this book. Silk threads have a high sheen and will add a luxurious touch to your work. Some are easier to use than others and the laundering requirements of the finished article should be taken into consideration when choosing to use silk. Always remember that you should wash the article according to the most delicate threads used. For example, silk embroidery of any kind worked on a towel will require the towel to be washed as if it were silk. Cotton threads would be a better choice for the embroidery.

KANAGAWA SILK THREAD

A beautiful smooth thread with a very firm twist.

- No. 16 Thread — Buttonhole Twist (or Kanagawa 1000). Available in a good range of colours. A single strand is equivalent to 3 strands of stranded cotton. Available on 20 metre cards.
- No. 30 Thread — Silk Stitch. Equivalent to 2 strands of stranded cotton. A limited colour range is available on 50 metre reels.
- No. 50 Thread. Machine embroidery weight on reels of 100 metres.

AU VER A SOIE SILK THREAD

- Soie D'Algere. A seven-strands stranded silk thread of which a single strand is slightly thicker than one strand of stranded cotton.
- Soie Perle. Similar to Kanagawa No. 16 Buttonhole Twist. Available on 50 metre reels.
- Soie Goblins. Similar to Kanagawa Silk Stitch. Also available on 50 metre reels.

OVER-DYED SILK THREAD

Mary Hart-Davies (Kacoonda) has a range of hand-dyed silk threads available in various thicknesses.

Another beautiful range of over-dyed stranded silk is available under the brand name of 'Waterlilies' from the Caron collection.

RAYON AND SYNTHETIC THREADS

Once again the choice is large. The main properties of these threads are that they are usually very springy, making them difficult to control, and have a very high sheen.

- Marlitt (or Decora). A 4 strand thread, difficult to handle when working with more than 2 strands.

- Isofil and Madeira — machine embroidery threads. Excellent threads for miniatures and jewellery but very fine and slippery.
- Brazilian Embroidery Threads. These threads are rayon and vary from fine silk-like thread, to heavy boucle and straw-like threads. They are very springy and come in fairly bright plain and variegated colours. Sources are very limited here in Australia.

Note that Down Under Designs (of Sydney, Australia) is one source for all the over-dyed threads imported from the USA, referred to in this chapter.

NEEDLES

Where possible I use straw or milliners needles for the flowers shown in the sampler. Tapestry (blunt point) or chenille (sharp point) will be required when working with heavier wools and Coton Perle No. 3 and 5. Crewel needles may also be used for needle painting projects.

FABRIC

Almost any type of fabric is suitable for most of the embroidery in this book, but see the special notes under project headings for more detail. The following points should be taken into consideration:

- Consideration should be given to necessary laundering if working designs on clothing, etc.
- Ironing is not recommended for the highly textured flowers such as roses, fuchsia and sweet pea. Make sure the base fabric will not require ironing.
- The heavier the pile of the background fabric, such as velvet or towelling, the heavier the thread required for the embroidery in order to achieve added texture.

EMBROIDERY HOOPS AND FRAMES

Refer to the instructions for individual projects for specific recommendations. Most of the work shown in this book does not require a frame, with the exception of the needle painting and the punchneedle.

TRANSFERRING A DESIGN ONTO FABRIC

One easy and very effective way to transfer the main design lines of a pattern onto all types of fabric accurately is to:

- Photocopy or trace the lines onto a sheet of paper.
- Position the design accurately on the fabric and carefully machine along the lines through the paper and the fabric. Use a matching thread and a medium-length stitch.
- Carefully tear away the paper and embroider over the machine lines.

Stitching through the paper pattern removes any stretch from the fabric and, as a result, this is an excellent way of marking a design accurately even on stretch fabrics.

If the design to be transferred is symmetrical, the paper pattern can be positioned on the wrong side of the work so that any fragments of paper remaining when the pattern is torn away will not be a problem. An asymmetrical design must be copied in reverse if worked from the back, or positioned on the front of the work and any paper fragments removed with a blunt needle after tearing away the paper.

This method of transferring a pattern is particularly useful if working on blanketing or pile fabrics that are difficult to mark accurately, and dark fabrics of any type that would normally require marking with a white chalk marker.

Water erasable and fadeable pens are very useful for marking the main features of a design onto the fabric. Remember to use the lightest touch possible to avoid marking the fabric too heavily. Restricting the design marks to the heaviest areas of embroidery will also ensure that these marks will be well hidden on the finished work. A double-ended water erasable pen is now available, with a fine tip at one end and a bold tip at the other.

Chalk pencils used for dressmaking are useful on dark fabrics. Make sure that they are well sharpened to give good results. Transfer pencils are available and should be used according to manufacturer's instructions.

CARE OF TEXTURED EMBROIDERY

Always wash embroidery according to the most delicate fibres used and do not use strong detergents on silk or rayon threads. Some of the flowers will be spoilt if flattened by ironing so take this into consideration when planning your project.

HELPFUL HINTS FOR LEFT-HANDED STUDENTS

There are more left-handed people around than there used to be and I think that teachers of embroidery can no longer ignore this so-called 'problem'. It takes time and concentration for a right-handed teacher to be able to demonstrate for left-handed students.

Fortunately, I find students very patient and appreciative of efforts to understand their problems and it can be very worthwhile to try to master the techniques their way.

The following points may help both teachers and students to reverse the techniques described in the following pages.

- Remember that not only is the needle held in the opposite hand but the direction of the thread must be altered as well. For example, if a right-hander has the thread on the left of the needle then the left-hander must put the thread to the right of the needle.

- If the right-handed worker is working from left to right, either in a straight line or a circle (clockwise), the left-hander will work from right to left in a line or a circle (anti-clockwise).

- Starting positions for left-handers are normally opposite to those for right-handers.

- Try using a mirror positioned as shown in the diagram to convert the diagrams to left-handed techniques.

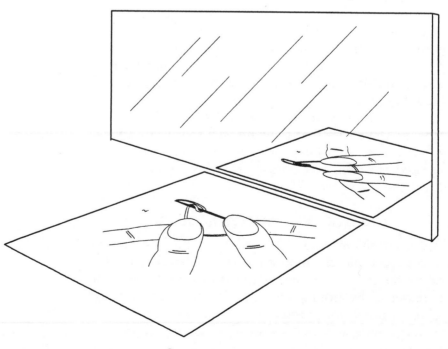

Fig 1-1

CHAPTER 2

STITCHES

Instructions on how to work the following stitches are given in this chapter:

1. Detached buttonhole stitch
2. Double-sided detached buttonhole stitch
3. Knotted loop stitch
4. Palestrina or double knot stitch
5. Bullion lazy daisy stitch
6. Colonial knot
7. Feather stitch
8. Pistil stitch
9. Couching
10. Ladder stitch
11. Stem or outline stitch
12. Fly stitch
13. Lazy daisy stitch
14. Portuguese stem stitch
15. Twisted chain
16. Long-legged twisted chain
17. Blanket stitch
18. Bullion stitch
19. Long-legged bullion stitch
20. Straight stitch
21. Raised stem band
22. French knot
23. Coral stitch

DETACHED BUTTONHOLE STITCH

(also known as cast on stitch)

This is a very versatile stitch and has been used for six of the flowers shown on the sampler on the colour pages.

Once you have mastered the technique of the stitch it is easier to work than bullion stitch and as equally effective, if not more so, than bullion stitch.

The thickness of the thread used and the size of the needle chosen will have a direct result on the size of the stitches. A straw or milliners needle will give the best results. Large-eyed needles will distort the stitches as they are pulled through the wraps and affect the evenness of the petals.

I recommend Coton Perle No. 8 as a good thread with which to practise using a No. 4 or 5 needle.

TO WORK A DETACHED BUTTONHOLE STITCH

Secure the thread with a small back stitch where it will be hidden under the flower centre, or a small knot may be used.

- Bring the needle up through the fabric at point A.
- Take a back stitch going down at B and back out at A, taking care not to pierce the thread at point A or to pull the needle right through the fabric. (Refer to flower instructions for stitch lengths, etc.)
- Slip the first finger of your right hand into the thread loop (diag. 1).
- Hold the thread over the thumb nail and across the middle finger of the right hand to tension the thread as you twist the loop and slide it onto the needle (diag. 2).
- Pull the thread until the loop tightens around the needle, making sure the loop slides to fit snugly at the point where the needle emerges through the fabric. (The knot created is a half hitch.)
- Repeat until the required number of loops have been worked onto the needle, making sure that each one fits snugly beside the previous one. There should be no gaps and no overlapping loops.
- Pull the needle through the fabric gently holding the loops between the finger and thumb of the left hand. Tighten the thread until the loops fill the length of the core thread.
- Anchor the stitch by passing the needle to the back of the work at point B. For loop stitches, used for petals, A and B are close together and to form the stitch into a cup shape, as required for some flowers:
- Pull the base of the stitch in closer by stitching together the first and last knot, as shown in diagrams 5, 6 and 7.

POINTS TO REMEMBER

- The shape of the finished stitch will be governed by

the length of the foundation back stitch and the number of loops worked onto the needle.

- Tighten the core thread carefully so that the loops fill the thread sufficiently. Too few loops worked for the size of stitch required will result in a loose floppy stitch that will not retain the shape of the flower.

- Care must be taken not to pull the back stitch too tight as you lay the stitch or the base fabric will pucker. This is most likely to happen if there are too few loops worked onto the needle.

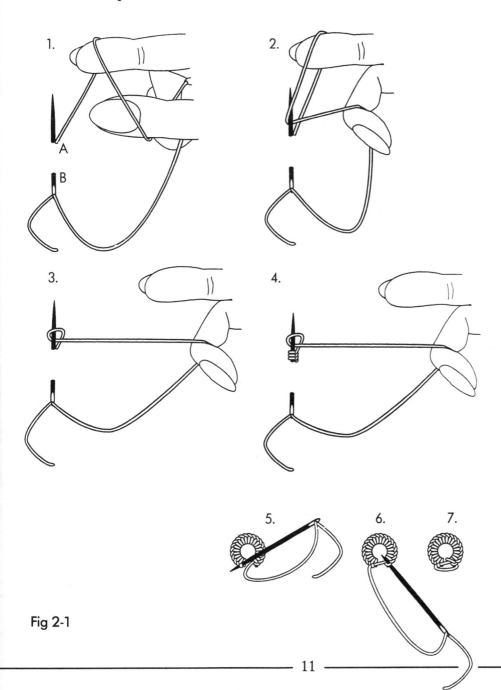

Fig 2-1

DOUBLE-SIDED DETACHED BUTTONHOLE STITCH

- Thread the needle with a long thread and knot the two cut ends together to form a double thread.
- Bring the needle up at point A, back stitch to B and up again at A. Bring the point of the needle out at point A between the two threads so that one lays on each side of the needle (diag. 1). Do not pull the needle right through the fabric.
- Work one loop with the right hand as described for detached buttonhole stitch, with the thread on the right side of the needle.
- Work a second loop using the left-hand thread in the left hand, pulling the knot to the left side of the needle (diag. 2 and 3).
- Work alternate right- and left-hand loops up the needle for the required length.
- Hold the loops gently in the left thumb and first finger as you pull the needle through the fabric.
- Ease the loops down, tighten the core thread carefully and anchor the stitch by passing the needle to the back of the work at point B (diag. 4).

The 'points to remember' listed on page 10 for the Detached Buttonhole Stitch also apply to this stitch.

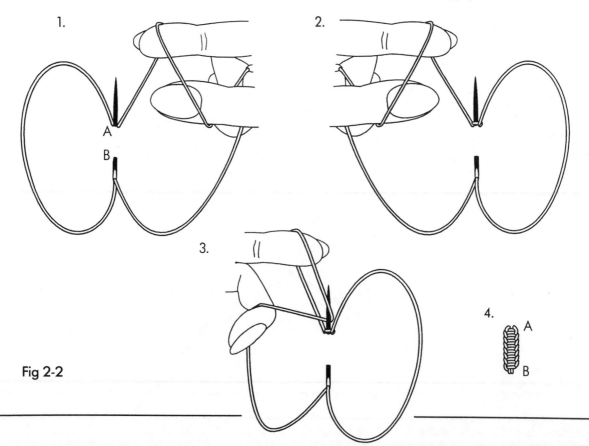

Fig 2-2

KNOTTED LOOP STITCH

This stitch will be easier to work to an even tension if the fabric is held taut in a hoop.

- Bring the needle up at point A. Form a small loop with the thread, holding it in place under the left thumb.

- Slide the needle under the thread close to point A and pull through gently until the loop of thread is of the desired size.

- Anchor the loop by passing the needle to the back of the work just inside the loop made and close to point A (diag. 2). Do not pull the knot too tight at this point or the loop may slide.

- Bring the needle up to the right of the completed loop and in line with the outer edge of that loop.

- Pass the needle through the finished loop to link the stitches together as you form the next loop (diag. 3).

- Slide the needle under the thread at point A, adjusting the size of the loop carefully to match the previously worked loop. Pass the needle to the back of the work at point A as before.

- When working this stitch into a circle, the final loop of each row must be linked by passing the needle through the stitches to the right and left of the loop being worked (diag. 4).

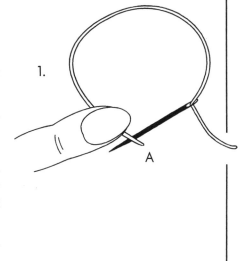

1.

A

2.

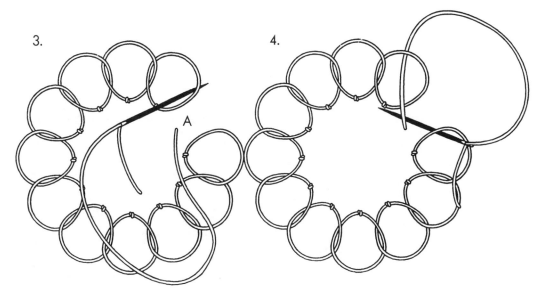

3.

A

4.

Fig 2-3

PALESTRINA OR DOUBLE KNOT STITCH

(The outline stitch illustrated in colour on the sampler)

If possible use a tapestry needle for this stitch to avoid splitting the working thread or picking up threads from the background fabric. If piercing the base fabric is too hard with a blunt needle, use a sharp needle but lead with the needle eye instead of the point when working under the stitches. Note that the needle must always pass from the top downwards when working over the bar stitch.

- Working from left to right, come up at point A on the line to be covered, take a small vertical stitch entering the fabric above the design line at B and bring the needle up below the line at C (diag. 1). Pull the needle through and tighten the thread to form a small bar stitch. The distance between points B and C will depend on the thickness of the threads used and the texture required.

- Keeping the thread to the right, slide the needle under the bar stitch from above and pull through (diag. 2).

- Allowing the thread to form a loop below the stitch, pass the needle under the bar stitch a second time, working through the top corner of the bar above the stitch just completed. Pull it through, keeping the needle on top of the thread loop (diag. 4).

- To work a line of these stitches, repeat the stitch as shown in diag. 4.

- To work single stitch for flower buds or sprays (as in 4A of the sampler on the colour pages); work a single stitch as described and finish by passing the needle to the back of the work at point D (diag. 5).

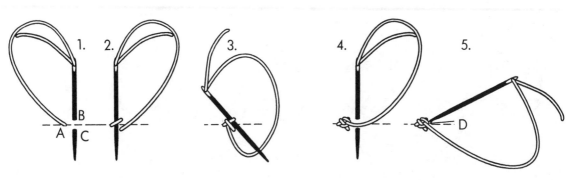

Fig 2-4

BULLION LAZY DAISY STITCH

This is a variation on the standard lazy daisy stitch. A small bullion stitch takes the place of the usual anchor stitch at the point of the petal. The shape of the petal or leaf will depend on the length of the bullion stitch used.

The secret of this stitch is to keep the thread taut at all times and tighten it firmly before anchoring the bullion.

Bring the needle up at point A, take it down again at point A and out at point B remembering that the bullion part of the stitch will extend beyond this point. Bring the thread under the point of the needle and wind it around the point of the needle two or three times. Lay the thread firmly to the base of the stitch, and hold in place gently by covering with the left thumb as you pull the needle through, keeping the thread close to the fabric and in line with the bullion stitch. Anchor the bullion stitch by returning the needle to the back of the fabric at the very end of the bullion (point C on the diagram).

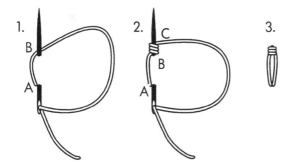

Fig 2-5

COLONIAL KNOT

(Also known as the candlewicking knot)

This knot is larger and firmer than a french knot. It is attractive as it sits up well on the fabric. The thread is wound around the needle in a figure eight.

Maintaining a flexible relaxed wrist is the key to easy execution of colonial knots allowing easy change of direction as the thread is picked up on the needle.

- Bring the needle up through the fabric and hold the thread between the thumb and first finger of the *left* hand, leaving a loop approximately 8 cm (3 inches) in length.
- Slide the first finger of the *right* hand under this loop and 'sandwich' the thread between this finger and the needle, which should be pointing away from you, and hook the needle under the thread (diag. 1).
- Turn the needle anti-clockwise through 180 degrees and hook the needle under the thread again (diag. 2).
- Return the needle in a clockwise direction to the original position and pass the needle back through the fabric close to, but not through, the original exit hole (diag. 3).

To produce well shaped, even knots always neaten the thread around the shaft of the needle, while the needle is held in a perpendicular position in the fabric, before completing the last step.

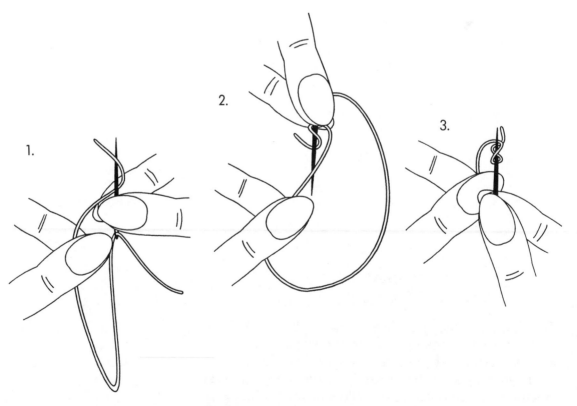

Fig 2-6

FEATHER STITCH

This stitch is useful for defining a shape that will be embroidered with a random selection of flowers. It can also be very useful as a background fill of fern type leaves.

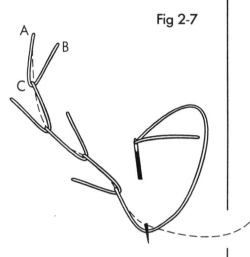

Fig 2-7

- Bring the needle up at A at the top of the line to be followed.

- Take the needle down through the fabric below this point and to the right of the line (point B).

- Slant the needle down slightly and bring it back to the surface on the line with the thread looped under the needle. Pull the needle through (point C).

- Repeat the stitch inserting the needle to the left of the centre line. Continue working down the line, alternating the stitches from side to side.

- This is a 'one-way' stitch, take care that all the stems point in the right direction on a design.

PISTIL STITCH

Always use an embroidery hoop or frame for this stitch.

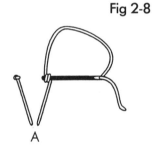

Fig 2-8

- Bring the needle up at point A.

- Pick up the thread once or twice around the needle.

- Return the needle to the back of the work the required distance from point A, pulling the thread taut around the needle as the needle is passed through the fabric.

COUCHING

It is easy to work fine stems with a natural curve using couching.

Very short stems can be worked with a single needle, however, for longer stems greater control is maintained by using two needles. The first needle carries a thread of suitable thickness for the required stem, usually one to four strands of embroidery thread. The second carries a single matching strand of thread. Always work this stitch in an embroidery frame.

Fig 2-9

- Using the first needle, come up at one end of the line to be covered and go down at the other. Anchor this needle out of the way.

- Bring the second needle up close to the starting point of the first thread and work tiny invisible straight holding stitches across the main thread, curving the main thread as desired.

LADDER STITCH

This is a simple and neat way to close seams left open for turning, and for invisibly joining two sections of work together.

Pick up a few threads of fabric along the seam line on one side then pick up the same distance along the seam line of the other side of the opening. The cross-over thread represents the rung of the ladder, the pick up sections the side supports.

As long as a strong enough thread is used, several stitches can be worked and then tightened really firmly to pull the two sides together securely.

Fig 2-10

STEM OR OUTLINE STITCH

- Bring the needle out at A, down at B and out again at C (where C is halfway between A and B) with the thread below the needle (diag. 1).
- Keeping the thread below the needle, take the needle down at D and back out at B (B is halfway between C and D), (diag. 2).

Note that stem stitch may curve more smoothly if worked with the thread above the needle, depending on the direction of the curve. Whether you choose to work with the thread above or below the needle it is important to keep it consistent in each line.

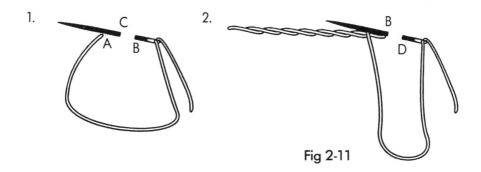

Fig 2-11

FLY STITCH

- Bring the needle up at A, then down at B and out again at C. Keep the thread from point A looped under the needle at C and pull the needle through (diag. 1).

- Anchor the stitch by passing the needle to the back of the work at D (diag. 2). Note that a small stalk can be created by moving point D further away from point C.

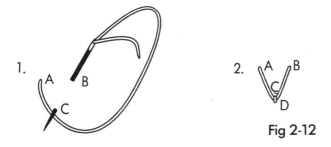

Fig 2-12

LAZY DAISY STITCH

- Bring the needle up at A, take it back down at A and out again at B, looping the thread under the point of the needle.

- Pull the needle through the fabric, tightening the thread gently. Anchor with a small stitch at the point of the stitch.

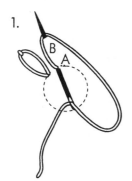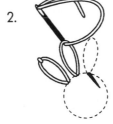

Fig 2-13

PORTUGUESE STEM STITCH

A lovely stitch with a cord-like texture based on the more familiar stem stitch which many readers will know. If possible use a tapestry needle when working this stitch.

- Working from the bottom up and stitching directly over the marked design lines, bring the needle up at point A.
- Keeping the thread on the right-hand side of the needle, take the needle down at B and up again at C. The distances from A to C and B to C should be equal.
- With the thread below the needle pass the needle fom right to left between the straight stitch just formed and the fabric, keeping the thread between B and C (diag. 2). Gently tighten the thread around the straight stitch.
- With the thread above the needle, add a second wrap around the straight stitch below the first wrap and gently tighten as before (diag. 3).
- With the thread to the right of the needle, work another stem stitch from D to B (diag. 4). Wrap as before taking the first wrap around the single stitch between D and B and the second wrap around both threads between B and C (diag. 6).

Be careful not to pick up threads from the base fabric or thread when wrapping the thread around the straight stem stitches. The use of a tapestry needle should help prevent this occurring.

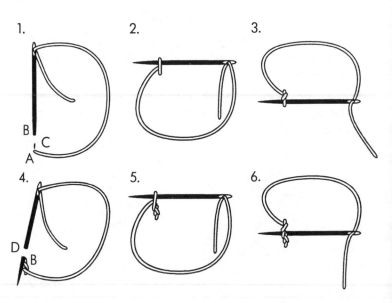

Fig 2-14

TWISTED CHAIN

- Work from the top of the design down directly over the line to be covered.
- Bring the needle up at A.
- Form a small anti-clockwise loop of thread and pass the needle down at B and out again at C. Note that point B is level with and close to A but to the left of A, so that the threads cross over at this point. The distance between A and C will vary according to the thickness of the thread being used. To maintain even stitching, distances between A, B and C must be consistent with every stitch. When working a continuous line, be sure to keep the needle very close to the design line at points B and D (diag. 1 and 2).

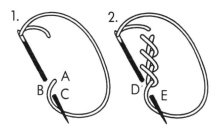

Fig 2-15

LONG-LEGGED TWISTED CHAIN

(Shown in colour at 4B on the sampler)

This is a pretty version of twisted chain stitch that can be used for flowers.

- Bring the needle up at A and form a loop of thread as for twisted chain. Pass the needle down at B and out at C (diag. 1).
  Note that point B is in line with point A but about 4 mm (just over ⅛ inch) to the left of A.
- Pull the needle through over the thread loop to tighten the stitch.
- Anchor the stitch by passing the needle to the back of the work at D (diag. 2).
  Note that the distance between points C and D may vary according to the shape of the flower being worked.

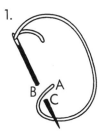

Fig 2-16

BLANKET STITCH

- Come up at A.
- Loop the thread anti-clockwise and take the needle down at B and back out at C over the looped thread.
- Tighten thread and repeat.

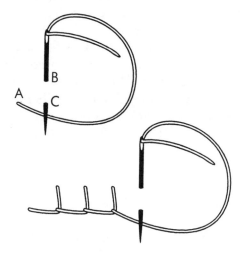

Fig 2-17

BULLION STITCH

- Bring the needle up at point A, down at point B and out again at point A. Do not pull the needle right through at this stage but wind the thread around the needle the necessary number of times to achieve the required length.
- Hold the wraps gently and pull the needle through. Tighten the wraps until they are even.
- Anchor the stitch by passing the needle to the back of the work at point B.
  For more detail on bullion stitch refer to my book *Bullion Stitch Embroidery* published by Sally Milner Publishing.

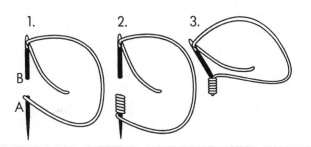

Fig 2-18

LONG-LEGGED BULLION STITCH

*(Used for the dividing lines on the sampler
on the colour pages)*

- Come up at A, down at B and back out at A. Do not pull the needle through at this time (diag. 1).
- Pick up the thread at A and wind it around the point of the needle until the wraps on the needle equal the length of the stitch between A and B.
- Hold the wraps lightly between the thumb and finger of the left hand and gently pull the needle through. Tighten the thread until the wraps are snug against the fabric.
- Carry the needle forward to C and back stitch to D. C to D is equal to A to B in length with a short space between B and D.
- Wrap the needle again using the thread from the end of the previous stitch.

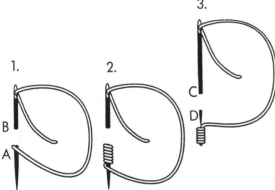

Fig 2-19

STRAIGHT STITCH

- Come up at A and go down at B.

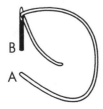

Fig 2-20

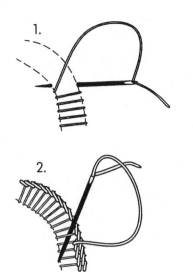

Fig 2-21

RAISED STEM BAND

This stitch is used extensively in needle painting and can be used to create wonderful texture. It can be worked with or without padding according to preference and both methods have been detailed for the picture illustrated. Whether or not padding is used, the method of working is the same.

- Working on a frame, lay down horizontal stitches, as shown in diag. 1, across the area to be worked. These stitches should be firm (particularly for the longer stitches) and about 1 to 2 mm ($^1/_{16}$ inch) apart for the work detailed in this book.

- Starting at the bottom, work stem stitch over the horizontal stitches, picking up each straight stitch in turn. Note! Pick up the thread only. Do not pick up the background fabric or padding if used. A size 26 tapestry needle is very suitable for this work.

FRENCH KNOT

- Pick up the thread with the needle (diag. 1).
- Turn the needle clockwise over the thread held in the left hand. Pass the needle back through the fabric close to, but not through, the original exit point (diag. 2).
Pull down gently on the thread as the needle is passed to the back of the work. This is essential for neat compact knots.

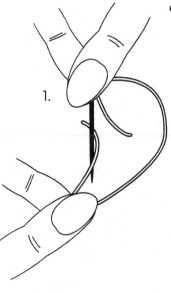
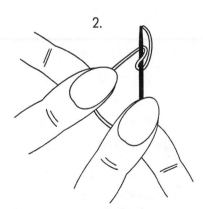

Fig 2-22

CORAL STITCH

(Used to frame the cover picture)

- Working from right to left, pull the needle through at A and lay the thread over the line to be followed.
- Looping the thread below the line, make a small vertical stitch from B to C, bringing the needle out over the top of the looped thread.
- Tighten the thread around the needle gently and pull the needle through.
- Repeat to form a line.

Note that spacing between stitches should be even and the distance between B and C will determine the size of the knot.

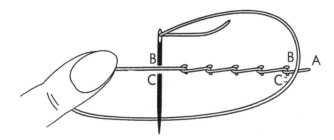

Fig 2-23

CHAPTER 3

FLOWERS

The construction of flowers as depicted on the sampler are described in this chapter. The sampler is reproduced in colour to the original worked size to give a clear indication of the size variation that can be achieved using various threads.

In the accompanying stitch placement diagrams, bold lines are used to indicate the stitch placement being described, whereas lighter lines and broken lines show previous completed steps. Coton Perle No. 8 is a good thread to practise with for most of these flowers.

ROSES

(Illustrated in colour at 1A on the sampler)

These roses are worked in detached buttonhole stitch, see page 9. They may be worked in a variety of threads, the type of thread chosen determining the size of the finished rose.

- The step-by-step illustration (fig. 3-1) is worked in two shades of Coton Perle No. 8 using a straw or milliners needle.
- Work a 10 wrap detached buttonhole stitch picking up 2 or 3 threads of the fabric for the base stitch (diag. 1).
- Pull the base of the stitch close by stitching together with a tiny straight stitch before passing the needle to the back of the work between the anchor points (see Detached Buttonhole Stitch, Chapter 2 fig. 2-1, diags. 5, 6 & 7).
- Work four 12 wrap overlapping stitches around the centre stitch (diag. 2).
- Change to a paler shade of thread and work a circle of six 12 wrap overlapping stitches around the outer edge of the first circle (diag. 3).

The roses shown on the bottom row of 1A on the sampler are all worked with the same number of wraps on the needle, as detailed above. The variation in size results from the choice of thread and the size of needle.

Far left — 1 strand of Paternayan Persian wool
Centre — 1 strand of DMC Flower thread
Far right — single strand of Isafil machine embroidery thread.

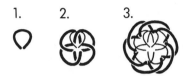

Fig 3-1

HIBISCUS

(Illustrated in colour at 1B [top row] on the sampler)

- Draw a tiny circle as shown in fig. 3-2, diag. 1.
- Work five 15 wrap overlapping stitches around the edge of the circle.
- Fill the centre with colonial knots worked with two strands of DMC stranded cotton in a contrasting colour.
- Add a small bead for the centre stamen. With a single strand of yellow thread in a fine needle, come up through the centre of the flower. Thread the bead onto the needle and back stitch through the bead, anchoring to the thread, before returning the needle to the back of the work through the centre of the flower. Back stitch the thread carefully to finish off, taking care not to pull the loop too tightly.

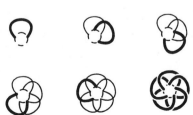

Fig 3-2

FUCHSIA AND LEAVES

(Illustrated in colour at 1B [bottom row] on the sampler)

- Work steps 1 and 2 as detailed for the Hibiscus but with 25 wraps for each petal (fig. 3-3, diag. 1).

- Using a single strand of stranded cotton work four or five pistil stitches hanging down from the centre (diag. 2).

- Fold the top petals down over the centre and stitch into a bell shape using matching thread, taking tiny stab stitches over the edges of the petals to shape the flower.

- With contrasting thread work a cluster of four or five straight stitches from the top of the bell towards the stem (diag. 3).

- Work three sepals in double-detached buttonhole stitch with 20 loops on the needle, from the top of the bell towards the stem (diag. 4).

- Using two strands of green thread, work a cluster of four straight stitches from the top of the pink cluster in the direction of the main stem (about half the length of the pink cluster). Complete by joining the flower to the main stem with a single straight stitch.

- Add buttonhole stitch leaves as follows:
  — Work two detached buttonhole stitches with 6 wraps on each side by side. Sew the tips of these stiches together at the outer end.
  — Work two more stitches of 10 wraps around the outside of the 6 wrap stitches. Sew the stitches together to form a point at the outer tip of the leaf.

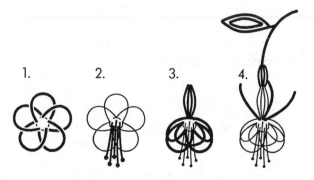

1.   2.   3.   4.

Fig 3-3

DAISIES

(Illustrated in colour at 2A on the sampler)

Large blue daisy was worked in Minnamurra Perle No. 8 (20).

- Mark a small circle for the centre, approximately 2 mm ($\frac{1}{16}$ inch) in diameter (fig. 3-4, diag. 1).
- Stitches are about 7 mm (just over ¼ inch) in length with 12 wraps.
- Work four stitches starting at the outer edge of the marked circle at 12, 3, 6 and 9 o'clock (diag. 2).
- Fill each gap with three stitches to complete the daisy.
- Fill the centre with colonial knots worked with one strand of flower thread or two of stranded cotton.
- The cream daisy is worked in the same way using DMC Flower thread.

To create a small daisy use a finer thread and start with a smaller centre (a single dot) work the marker stitches, about 5 mm ($\frac{3}{16}$ inch) long and 10 wraps, and finish with a single colonial knot for the centre. The tiny daisy spray is worked with two strands of Minnamurra Threads stranded cotton.

- Work a spray of uneven feather stitching in a single strand of green.
- Picking up 1 or 2 threads for the base stitch work 12 wraps on the needle and pull through firmly to form a circle. Pass the needle to the back of the work to close the circle.
- Work a tiny holding stitch across the edge of the stitch on the opposite side of the circle.
- Finish with a colonial knot in the centre of each flower worked in a single strand of stranded cotton.

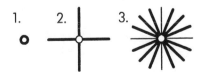

Fig 3-4

SWEET PEAS

(Illustrated in colour at 2B on the sampler)

Worked in Minnamurra stranded cotton (four strands) in colour number 20. Coton Perle is a very suitable alternative.

- Work two detached buttonhole stitches with 8 wraps for the centre. Stitch these two stitches together at both ends to make them stand up (fig. 3-5, diag. 1).

- Work a 24 wraps stitch around the first two stitches, taking care not to pull the stitch too tight.

- Work a stitch of 32 wraps around the edge of the previous stitches, adjusting the tension carefully so that the stitches just overlap.

- Stitch the last two stitches down on the fabric at the centre top of the flower (diag. 3).

- Shape the base of the flower by pulling the petals together towards the centre with a tiny holding stitch (as shown in chapter 2, fig. 2-1, diag. 5, 6 & 7).

Fig 3-5

BUD

(Illustrated in colour at 2B [top row, far right] on the sampler)

- Work two stitches of 10 wraps side by side and stitch the tip of the bud together.

- Work three stitches of 6 wraps in green, one on either side of the bud and one in between the first two stitches.

- Stitch the outer green stitches together at the base of the bud to improve the shape.

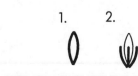

Fig 3-6

BELL FLOWER SPRAY

(Illustrated in colour at 2B [lower right] on the sampler)

- Couch a stem into place (fig. 3-7).
- Work a single 15 wraps detached buttonhole stitch at the tip of the stem. Pull the edges together at the top to shape the petal.
- Work two 15 wraps overlapping stitches and stitch the edges together at the top to shape (diag. 1).
- Work four or five overlapping stitches of 15 wraps around a small circle. Fold over and stitch as for Fuchsias.
- Work straight stitch in green across the top of the petals to join the flowers to the stem.
- The long straight leaf is worked with double-sided buttonhole stitch.

1.   2.

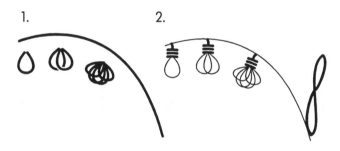

Fig 3-7

DAHLIA

(Illustrated in colour at 3A on the sampler)

Worked in knotted loop stitch, these flowers work well in wool or thread. The stitch must be worked inwards from the outside and it is very important to judge the size of the circle to allow sufficient room for the required number of rows.

Worked in a hoop using Coton Perle No. 8.

- Draw a circle approximately 8 mm (⁵⁄₁₆ inch) diameter (fig. 3-8).
- Work a row of knotted loop stitch around the outer edge of the circle.
- Work a second row just inside the first row working the knots very close to the outer row and making the loops equal in size to those of the first row. The top of each loop will lay just inside the top of the loops on the previous row.
- Continue working in circles until the centre is filled. The rows must be packed closely to make a dense flower.

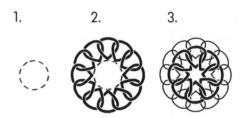

Fig 3-8

BLOSSOM

(Illustrated in colour at 3A [top right] on the sampler and the centre flower on the cover)

This is worked in the same way as the dahlia for the first two rows and the centre is then filled with colonial knots.

Worked in Coton Perle No. 12 for the small flowers on the sampler and in tapestry wool for the white flower on the cover.

WOOL ROSES

(Illustrated in colour at 3B on the sampler)

These flowers have been worked in Kacoonda variegated wool and Coton Perle No. 8.

- Using Coton Perle, work a single colonial knot for the centre.
- Work six or seven colonial knots in a tight circle around the centre knot (fig. 3-9).

- Work a second circle around the outside of the centre cluster. It is important to pull the knots of this row in towards the centre of the flower by working the needle at an angle, sliding it in and out under the edge of the previous row. This helps to push the centre of the flower up, giving the finished flower a more rounded look.

- With the wool, work two circles of stem stitch around the circle of knots, working with the thread above the needle and leaving the stitches slightly looped. Adjust the distance between the rows according to the thickness of the thread used. Do not cramp the stitches too much.

- Divide the outer edge into 8 as shown in diag. 2.

- Work two or three back stitches between each mark to complete the flower.

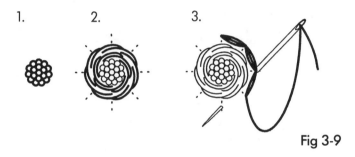

1.   2.   3.

Fig 3-9

WOOL ROSE BUDS

(Illustrated in colour at 3B on the sampler)

- Couch stems with fine wool or thread.

- Work the rose buds with four or five straight stitches using the same hole to start and finish all stitches (fig. 3-10).

- Using fine green wool, work one or two straight stitches halfway up the centre of the bud.

- Starting on the left side of the bud, work a fly stitch around the base of the bud (diag. 2).

- Work a second fly stitch directly over the first one if required.

- Work fly stitch leaves. Start with a straight stitch for the top half of the leaf. Continue down the leaf working three or four fly stitches.

1.   2.

Fig 3-10

BUD SPRAYS

(Illustrated in colour at 4A on the sampler)

These buds are worked in a single palestrina knot stitch. (See page 14.)

- Couch stems into place.
- Scatter single palestrina knot stitches amongst the stems.
- Join the buds to the stems by working a fly stitch around the base of each knot in a single strand of green.
- Add leaves in bullion lazy daisy stitch.

LONG-LEGGED TWISTED CHAIN FLOWERS

(Illustrated in colour at 4B on the sampler)

The flowers on the sampler have been worked in metallic thread, Coton Perle No. 8 and mohair wool (brushed to give a puff ball effect).

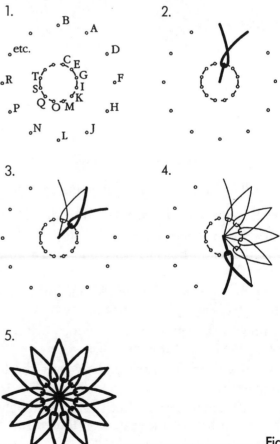

Fig 3-11

This flower is a little difficult to judge accurately at first but one or two practice runs should sort out any problems.

- Mark a small circle about 5 mm (⅕ inch) diameter and mark the centre of that circle (*not* shown actual size in fig. 3-11).

- Commence stitching about 5 mm outside the edge of the circle. Work a twisted chain stitch starting at A on the outer ring.

- Take the needle down at B and out again at C on the inner circle. Anchor the stitch by passing the needle to the back through the centre of the circles.

- Bring the needle up at D, down at A and out E. Anchor this stitch in the centre.

- Repeat for F, D and G, then H, F and I etc.

CHAPTER 4

EMBROIDERY DESIGNS

Designs pictured in this book are detailed in this section. Thread colours listed are those used in the original designs. Suggestions are given for using the designs in other ways.

Flowers used in the designs are depicted with the symbols detailed and instructions for working each flower will be found in Chapter 3.

Large and Small Dahlia
3A on sampler

Large Wool Daisy
3A on sampler

Blossom
3A on sampler

Roses
1A on sampler

Tiny Roses
1A on sampler

Hibiscus
1B on sampler

Fuchsia
1B on sampler

Daisies
2A on sampler

Tiny Daisy Spray
2A on sampler

Sweet Pea
2B on sampler

Bud
2B on sampler

Bell Flowers
2B on sampler

 Wool Roses
3B on sampler

Straight Stitch Wool Rose Buds
3B on sampler

Bullion Lazy Daisy Leaves and Buds

Detached Buttonhole Stitch Leaves
— Single Stitch
— Double Stitch

Fly Stitch Leaves

Single Palestrina Stitch Buds
or Colonial Knots

COVER PIECE — SUITABLE FOR A PICTURE

THREADS

Thread Description	Colour	No.	Strands	Embroidery
DMC stranded cotton	green	523	6	main stems
DMC stranded cotton	brown	3790	6	main stems and frame
Coton Perle No. 8	pale yellow	745		large and small dahlia
Coton Perle No. 8	yellow	744		large and small dahlia
Coton Perle No. 8	cream	712		hibiscus
DMC stranded cotton	pink/red	326	2	hibiscus centre
Minnamurra Thread	blue/pink	20		sweet pea and large and
Coton Perle No. 8				small daisies
Leah's Over-dyed	pink	12		bell flowers,
Coton Perle No. 8 or				fuchsia and
DMC Coton Perle No. 8		776		small palestrina buds
DMC Flower Thread	ecru			fuchsia and blossom
DMC stranded cotton	pink/brown	3773	2	blossom centres
DMC Flower Thread	yellow	2745,		small roses,
		2743 and		large palestrina buds
or		2742		and flower centres
Leah's Over-dyed	yellow	10		
Coton Perle No. 12				
Paternayan	pale pink	934	1	large roses
Persian Yarn	deep pink	932	1	rose buds
Appletons Crewel	olive green	3403		fly stitch leaves
Coton Perle No. 8	green	3346		double leaves
DMC stranded cotton	green	3053	3	single leaves
Appletons Tapestry	off white	992		white daisy

- From fig. 4-1a, mark main stem lines and frame outline by machine onto the base fabric backed with Pellon.
- Couch the main stems into place.
- Starting with the largest flowers in the centre and working towards the outer small sprays, embroider the picture as detailed fig 4-1b.
- Fill in the frame lines in coral stitch.

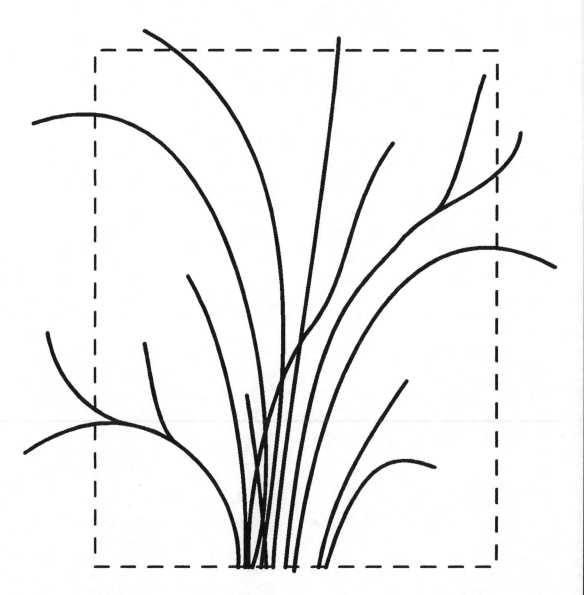

Fig 4-1a

SAMPLER SHOWING CONSTRUCTION OF FLOWERS

BLANKETS AND KNEE RUGS IN WOOL

WASHABLE FABRIC BOXES

PARTITIONED JEWEL BOXES FOR SPECIAL OCCASION GIFTS

CHARMING TEDDY BEARS IN PUNCHNEEDLE EMBROIDERY BY PAT KANE

CHATELAINE, PIN CUSHION AND NEEDLE BOX

Ring Pillow and Jewellery

Fuchsias worked on a purchased Linen Handbag

'Cosy Carry'—A Stole-type Garment with useful Large Pockets

Needle-painting Techniques worked in miniature for a Pendant

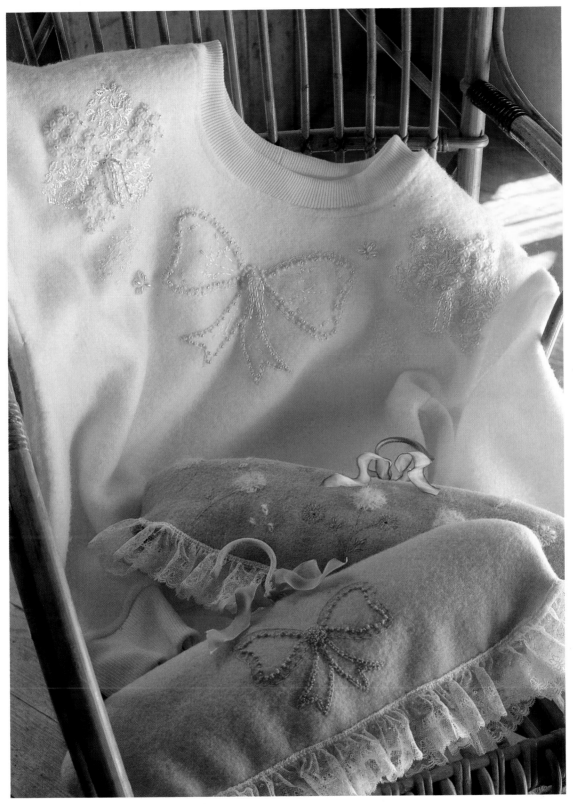

IDEAS FOR WOOL EMBROIDERY. SWEATER BY HELEN JANOCHA

BUSH SCENE NEEDLE PAINTING BY JOYCE MCKEE

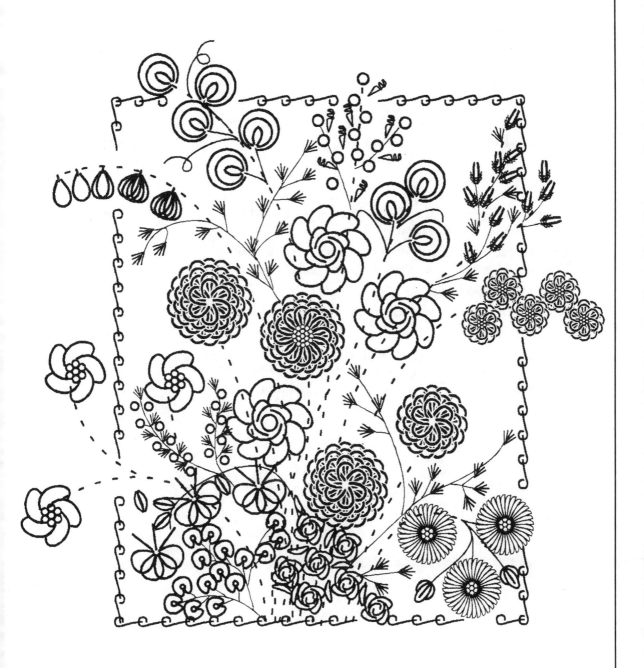

Fig 4-1b

HEART — BOX TOP DESIGN

THREADS

Thread Description	Colour	No.	Strands	Embroidery
Kreinik Balger Cord	silver	001C	1	feather stitching
DMC stranded cotton	green	3364	1	feather stitching
Coton Perle No. 8	green	3346		leaves
Coton Perle No. 8	pale pink	818		roses
	and pink	776		
DMC stranded cotton	white		2	baby's breath
Kreinik Balger Medium (No. 16) Braid	silver	001		silver ribbons

- From fig. 4-2, mark the design lines and lid outline by machine (reference page 6).
- Outline the heart shape with silver feather stitching overlaid with a second row of green feather stitch.
- Work roses and leaves.
- Work baby's breath in colonial knots.
- Work silver ribbons in long-legged bullion stitch.

This design can be enlarged and worked in heavier threads on a cushion, or in wool on a blanket. Dahlias, daisies, blossom or hibiscus can all be substituted for the roses.

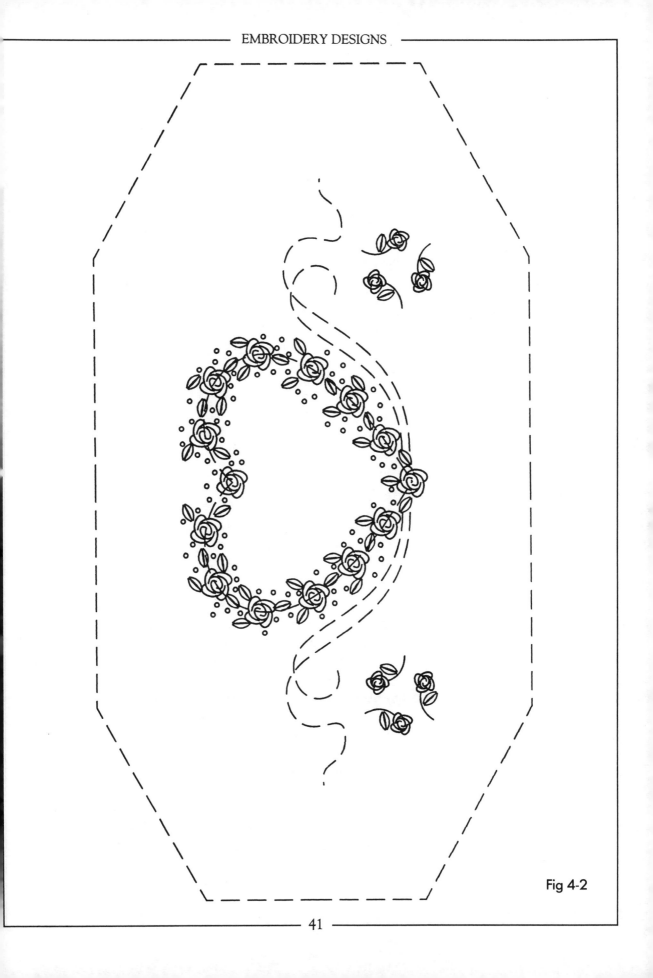

Fig 4-2

HEXAGONAL BOX TOP

THREADS

Thread Description	Colour	No.	Strands	Embroidery
Marlitt	magenta	815	4	large flowers back petals
			3	large flowers front petals
Kanagawa silk No. 16	dark green	113		leaves
Button hole twist (Kanagawa 1000)	med. green or	114		leaves and stems
DMC stranded cotton	dark green	3051		
	med. green	3053		
Jyava Ra Rame metallic thread or	gold	22		flower centres and outlining
Kreinik Metallic	gold	002P		
Caron Waterlilies or	cream	78	1	small cream flowers
DMC Flower thread	ecru			
Au Ver a Soie silk	blue	134	1	blue cluster flowers

- From fig. 4-3, mark the design lines and lid outline by machine (page 6).
- Work stems in Portuguese stem stitch using dark green thread.
- Outline each stem in stem stitch with gold thread.
- Large flowers are worked in detached buttonhole stitch working 35 wraps for each of the back three petals and 20 wraps for the two front side petals. Anchor each stitch in place with a holding stitch through the centre stitch of each petal.
- Join flowers to the main stem with satin stitch.
- Leaves are worked in two shades of green worked in the same way as the flower buds (page 30, 2B on the sampler).
- Work small cream flowers as for hibiscus flowers with 25 wraps. Fill the centre with a single colonial knot using two strands of Marlitt thread surrounded by colonial knots in gold metallic thread.
- Work clusters of tiny daisy stitches with 25 wraps. Finish centres with a gold colonial knot.

The design for this box was based on the design of the print fabric chosen for the box. This design would also be effective on an evening bag, cushions and clothing such as the yoke of a vest or jacket, or the collar of a dress.

Fig 4-3

CREAM RECTANGULAR BOX

THREADS

Thread Description	Colour	No.	Strands	Embroidery
DMC stranded cotton	dark green	3052	6	stems
			3	buds
Minnamurra Coton Perle No. 8	yellow/pink	50		roses and buds
Jyava Ra Rame metallic thread	gold	22		bow outlining
taffeta ribbon 5 mm (¼ inch) wide	green			bow

- From fig. 4-4, mark the design lines and box top by machine (page 6).
- Pin and tack the ribbon to cover the bow shape. Edge stitch in place by hand before working Portuguese stem stitch in metallic thread along the edges. Alternatively edge stitch by machine using metallic thread if desired.
- Couch stems in place.
- Work roses and buds.

This design is suitable for enlargement and could be used on a cushion, blanket, or across the front of a sweater or 'sloppy joe'.

Fig 4-4

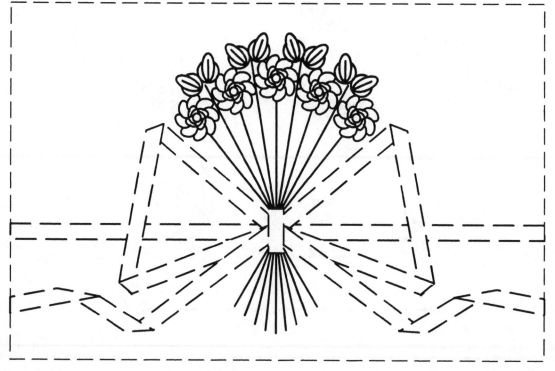

NEEDLE BOX

THREADS

Thread Description	Colour	No.	Strands	Embroidery
Coton Perle No. 8	apricot	353		line work
DMC Flower thread	ecru			daisies
Minnamurra				
Coton Perle No. 8	green	120		leaves
or stranded cotton	green	993		

gold beads and tiny gold charms as desired

- Photocopy the design (fig. 4-5) and transfer as detailed (page 6).
- Work the curved line in palestrina stitch.
- Work daisies in the Flower thread, finishing the centre with a gold bead.
- Work leaves with two stitches in detached button-hole stitch.
- Construct the box as instructed.
- Sew on tiny charms as an extra embellishment.

This design has been worked in finer threads on the scissor holder (where roses have been substituted for the daisies) and it would be suitable for collars or cuffs on blouses or lingerie. It can also be enlarged and worked in heavier threads for a bag.

Fig 4-5

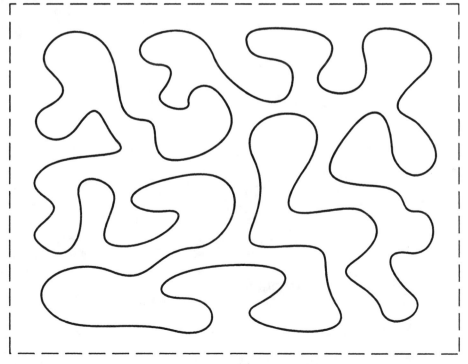

NAVY BLANKET

(Worked as a knee rug 110 cm x 80 cm [43 inches x 31½ inches])

THREADS

Thread Description	Colour	No.	Strands	Embroidery
Kacoonda wool thick	orange/pink	6F		heart outline and roses
Kacoonda wool fine	green	8E		leaves and stems
Coton Perle No. 8	yellow	742		flower centres
Kanagawa				
silk ribbon 4 mm	cream	156		buds
silk ribbon 2mm	green	31		buds and colonial knots

- Using figs. 4-6 and 4-7a, transfer the design to the blanket as described on page 6.
- Outline hearts using palestrina stitch and feather stitch as shown in the pattern.
- Work roses, rose buds and leaves (3B on the sampler) as shown in fig. 4-7b.
- Work cream silk ribbon buds in bullion lazy daisy stitch.

Fig 4-6

- Work two small straight stitches over the base of each bud in 2 mm green ribbon.
- Work French knots in green ribbon to complete the spray.
- Scatter single rose buds in wool over the centre of the blanket.

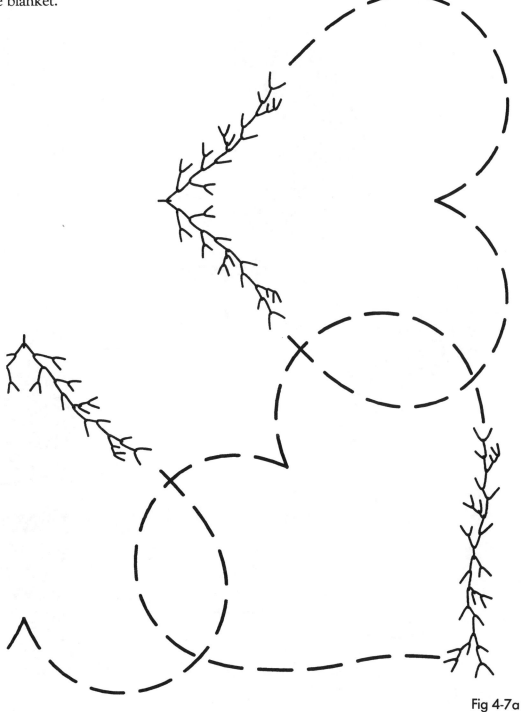

Fig 4-7a

Fig 4-7b

CREAM BLANKET

(Circle of hearts design on a 110 cm x 80 cm [43 inches x 31½ inches] blanket)

THREADS

Thread Description	Colour	No.	Strands	Embroidery
Pengouin Talisman silk/viscose knitting yarn	cream	001		heart outline and colonial knots
Paternayan Persian yarn	pink	931, 932 and 933		roses
	green	A604		
Rowan Botany 4 ply wool	blue	123		colonial knots
Kacoonda thin wool or	green	8C		stems and leaves
Appletons crewel	green	3505		
Coton Perle No. 8	yellow	742		flower centres

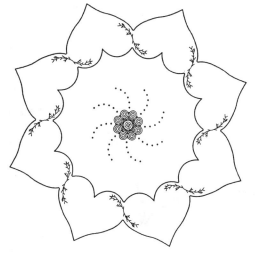

Fig 4-8

- Using figs. 4-8 and 4-9a, transfer the pattern to the blanket as described on page 6.
- Outline the hearts in Talisman knitting yarn with palestrina stitch.
- Work a spray of feather stitching in thin green wool for each rose spray.
- Work rose and rose buds using a single strand of Paternayan wool (3B on the sampler).
- Add colonial knots in blue and white.

Fig 4-9a

For the centre posy:

- Work a single rose for the centre.

- Using a single strand of green Paternayan wool, surround the rose with leaves worked in a single detached buttonhole stitch with 8 wraps for each leaf.

- Work 3 colonial knots in cream between the leaves.

- Work 8 roses around the outer edge and complete the posy by working colonial knots in cream along the outer design lines.

- Small rose sprays can be worked across the outer corners if desired.

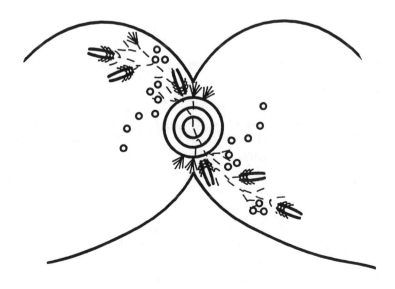

Fig 4-9b

BUTTERFLIES

Pictured on the Cosy Carry but also ideal for a blanket or sweater.

THREADS

These butterflies are pretty worked in variegated threads. If possible choose threads that are available in a variety of thicknesses, or stranded so that the thickness can be varied according to the size of the butterfly being worked.

The threads chosen for the butterflies illustrated are Kacoonda hand-dyed silk and wool.

Large butterfly

thick wool	3B upper wing outline
thick wool	8C lower wing outline
thick silk	3C upper wing veins
thick silk	8C lower wing veins

Toning beads approx. 4 mm (⅛ inch) diameter.

Medium butterfly

high twist silk	3C upper wing outline
high twist silk	8C lower wing outline
medium wool	3B upper wing veins
medium wool	8C lower wing veins

Toning beads approx. 2 mm (1/16 inch) diameter.

Small butterfly

fine wool	3B upper wing outline
fine wool	8C lower wing outline
fine silk	3C upper wing veins
fine silk	8C lower wing veins

All Butterflies:
DMC stranded cotton 611 for body and feelers and small piece of felt for body.

- Transfer design lines from fig. 4-10 as detailed on page 6.
- Work butterflies in palestrina stitch using beads to highlight the wing outline of the large butterfly and the veins of the medium butterfly. Stitch a bead in each 'cup' formed by the stitching. Note that other stitches that could be used for the outlining are: Portuguese stem stitch, long-legged bullion or coral stitch.
- Cut the appropriate size body shape out of felt. Using a single strand of DMC stranded cotton, sew in position with horizontal bars and cover with raised stem band (see page 24).
- Work feelers in stem stitch using a single strand of DMC stranded cotton.

Fig 4-10

SWEATER DESIGN BY HELEN JANOCHA

This design will look just as pretty on a blanket or cushion. See design shown in fig. 4-13.

THREADS

Thread Description	Colour	No.	Strands	Embroidery
Marlitt	cream	1212		
or				
Kanagawa silk thread				
No. 16 buttonhole twist	cream	16		equivalent to 4 strands of Marlitt
No. 30 silk stitch	cream	16		equivalent to 2 strands of Marlitt
DMC tapestry wool	ecru			
DMC stranded cotton	cream	712		
Coton Perle No. 5	cream	712		
Appletons crewel wool	off-white	992		

Beads: 4 mm (⅛ inch) diameter (Hotspotz no. RP70CR)
200 round and 44 oval pearls
Beading thread (Nymo) or equivalent
Size 9 straw needle or beading needle

- Helen marks the design on the back of the fabric in pencil then tacks around the outline to transfer the design to the right side. Her design (fig. 4-11) is also ideal for marking by machine as detailed on page 6. However, as the flower petal outline is not covered with embroidery, the machine stitching used for this outline should be a long stitch so that it can be removed after completion of the embroidery.

Fig 4-11

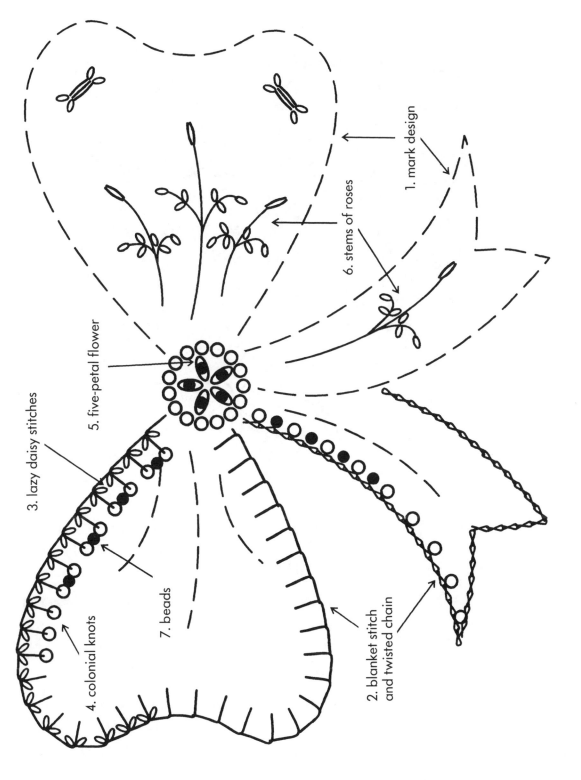

1. mark design

6. stems of roses

5. five-petal flower

3. lazy daisy stitches

4. colonial knots

7. beads

2. blanket stitch and twisted chain

Fig 4-12a

Fig 4-12b

Bow (fig. 4-12a)

- With Coton Perle No. 5 embroider
  - blanket stitch around the top of the bow spacing the stitches about 7 mm apart
  - twisted chain to outline the tails of the bow
  - lazy daisy stitches at the base of each blanket stitch.
- Using the DMC tapestry wool, embroider colonial knots
  - at the point of each blanket stitch
  - around the circle in the centre of the bow
  - 1 cm apart along the edge of the tails of the bow.
- Work a 5-petal lazy daisy flower in tapestry wool in the centre of the bow knot.
- Using two strands of Marlitt thread,

- couch stems for the roses along the marked lines
- couch small stems and attach lazy daisy leaves
- work two 14 wrap bullion stitches for each rose bud. Note that buds as shown at 2B on the sampler can be substituted here: work two centre stitches in the Appletons crewel wool and three small stitches with a single strand of the Marlitt.

- Attach beads between alternate colonial knots used on the bow outline, between each of the knots on the bow tail and in each lazy daisy stitch in the bow knot.

Flowers (fig. 4-12b)

- Using DMC tapestry wool, scatter 5-petal flowers in lazy daisy stitch in each alternate petal and one single flower in the flower centre.

- Using four strands of Marlitt thread work fly stitch leaves in different directions to cover the remaining petals.

- Sew beads to the centre of each flower.

Small Sprays of Bell Flowers (fig. 4-12c)

- Using two strands of the DMC stranded cotton,
  - feather stitch from point A
  - blanket stitch bell flowers onto alternate stems of feather stitch.

- Using two strands of the Marlitt,
  - work colonial knots along the base of the bell flowers
  - work two lazy daisy leaves onto every other stem.

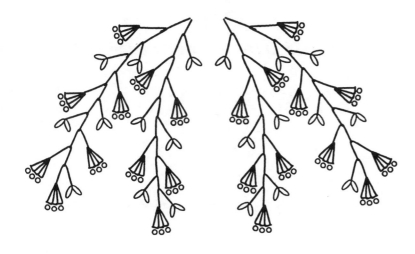

Fig 4-12c

The Butterfly (fig. 4-12d)

- Using the Coton Perle No. 5
  — work one 14 wrap bullion stitch for the body
  — embroider a double colonial knot for the head and two pistil stitches for antenna
  — work a double lazy daisy stitch for each wing if not using beads. For beaded wings, stitch two beads for front wings (one oval and one round) and one oval bead for each back wing. Allow space between top and bottom wings to allow final bullion stitches to sit properly.

- Using two strands of crewel wool, work a 45 wrap bullion stitch around the top wings starting at point A. Work 35 wrap bullion stitches around the lower wings. Couch each bullion at the halfway point to hold in place.

Tassels

Tassels can be added to the centre of the flowers and the bow

- Using strong thread (Nymo double), anchor the thread firmly to the work. Thread the required number of beads onto the thread and return the needle to the back of the work by threading it back through the centre of all the beads except the end bead where the thread is turned.

Fig 4-12d

Fig 4-13

COAT HANGER DESIGNS

PINK HANGER

(Sweater bow pattern reduced to 60 per cent of full size)

All embroidery was worked with two strands of Appletons crewel wool No. 943 together with small coloured pearl beads (Mill Hill colour no. 2004).

BLUE HANGER

Threads: Mohair wool in off-white and Jyava Ra Rame metallic gold thread no. 22.

- Long-legged twisted chain flowers in mohair are scattered over the surface, interspersed with smaller gold flowers in the same stitch worked with two strands of gold thread.
- Use two strands of gold thread to work stems in Portuguese stem stitch and leaves in double lazy daisy stitch.
- Single twisted chain stitches in mohair are scattered between the flowers.

FUCHSIA BAG

A ready-made handbag was used for this design (fig. 4-14). The bag, made of black linen with a thin padding under the area embroidered, was not difficult to work using detached buttonhole stitch.

When working on this type of project, a slightly padded surface will be easier to handle and a careful choice of stitches is recommended. For example, colonial knots are not easy to work in this situation. Starting threads must be buried in the fabric some distance from where you wish to start. A tiny back stitch can be used for added security where it is hidden under the embroidery.

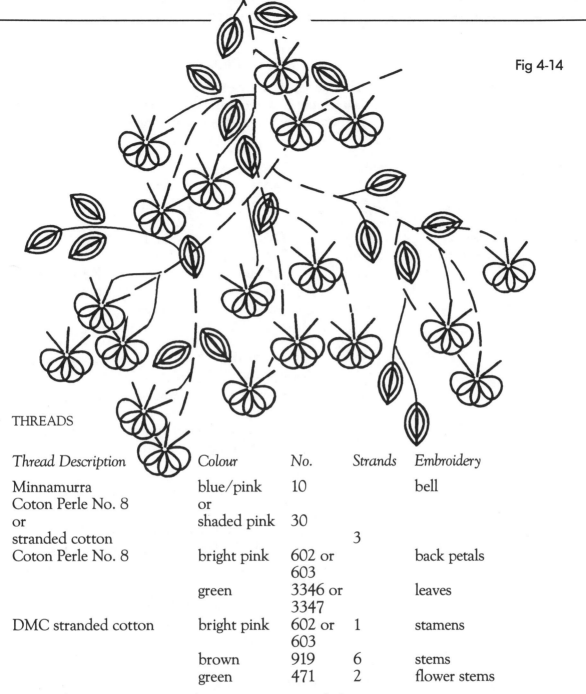

Fig 4-14

THREADS

Thread Description	Colour	No.	Strands	Embroidery
Minnamurra Coton Perle No. 8 or stranded cotton	blue/pink or shaded pink	10 30	3	bell
Coton Perle No. 8	bright pink green	602 or 603 3346 or 3347		back petals leaves
DMC stranded cotton	bright pink brown green	602 or 603 919 471	1 6 2	stamens stems flower stems

- Couch main stems into place to give a general shape to the design.
- Work clusters of flowers and leaves hanging from these stems. (See page 28 for detailed instructions.)

These fuchsias are very colourful and attractive but should not be used on any article that will require ironing as they are easily pushed out of shape. They are most suitable for picture work or articles such as the evening bag, padded hair bands and slides, or jewellery pieces.

PILLOW DESIGN

This design is a repeatable pattern that can be used to cover any area required. It is suitable for enlargement and can be worked effectively in heavier threads.

THREADS

Thread Description	Colour	No.	Strands	Embroidery
Coton Perle No. 8	cream	712		outline design
DMC stranded cotton	cream	712	2	all daisies
	yellow	744 and	1	mix strands for
		743	1	flowers centres
	green	523	2	leaves

- From fig. 4-15, outline the main design lines with Portuguese stem stitch.
- Work a daisy in two strands of stranded cotton at each intersection. Fill in the centres of the daisies with colonial knots, using one of each of the two yellows mixed together.
- Centre posy:
  — work a single daisy in knotted loop stitch for the centre
  — surround the centre flower with eight buds
  — surround the buds with eight flowers, alternating knotted loop stitch blossoms with detached buttonhole stitch daisies
  — fill in the centres of the flowers as before
  — add small leaves in detached buttonhole stitch between each of the daisies on the outer ring.

MINIATURE PIECE PICTURED ON THE BACK COVER

This piece is worked as a pendant using needle-painting techniques. The work is designed around a hand-crafted silver wombat button by Marylyn Verstraeten (artist in silver and gold).

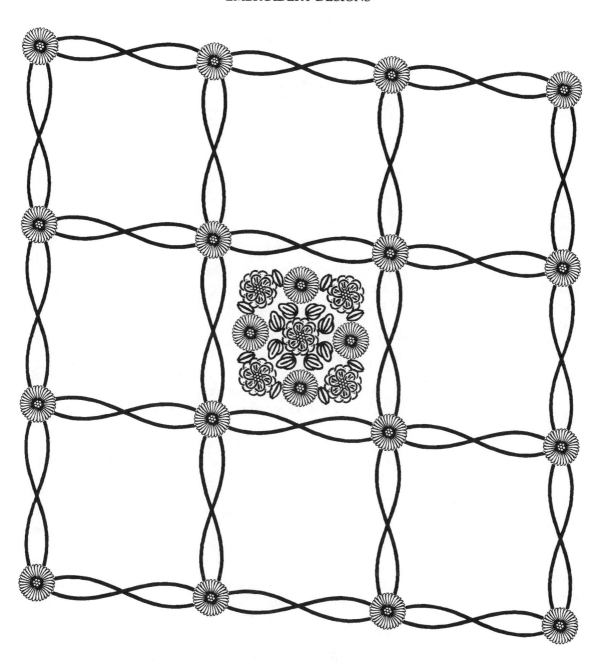

Fig 4-15

CHAPTER 5

PROJECTS

BOXES

All the boxes detailed in this section are made by hand and using a sewing machine. No glue is required during construction and plastic templates are used for stiffening, making the boxes washable, provided the fabric chosen for the box can be laundered.

A variety of shapes and sizes can be made using the basic method. Inserts such as partitioned trays add interest to jewellery or sewing boxes.

For large boxes, extra strength can be obtained by using the plastic sheet double for the templates and choosing a firm fabric, such as furnishing cotton, to work with.

The method of constructing the box is exactly the same whatever the shape or size. The basic principle is to make a strip of pockets into which the templates are fitted for the sides of the boxes and single pockets for the top and bottom of the box. All these pockets are constructed on the sewing machine with the final construction of the box being worked by hand.

Care must be taken to:

- Cut the templates accurately and label them to avoid confusion during construction

- Lay out the templates very carefully to mark the pocket sizes. A firm snug fit is essential for good results. Each pocket should be about 3 mm (⅛ inch) wider than the template to allow for the padding of the template.

- Firmly woven cotton fabrics are easiest for a beginner to work with. Once the technique has been mastered, silks, satins and synthetics are all suitable provided the weave is firm. Lighter weight fabrics are easier to handle for smaller boxes.

- When working embroidery on a box lid, back the fabric with Pellon and centre the design carefully. Always stitch the outline of the lid pocket when transferring the main design lines, as detailed on page 6. This outer line should include the extra pocket allowance mentioned above, as this stitching line is used when constructing the lid pocket after the embroidery is completed. *Note that all lid designs detailed in this book include the correct pocket allowance.*

- Trim the Pellon back to the seam line before turning the lid pocket.
- Trim all seams to approximately 9 mm (⅜ inch) and always cut the fabric away across the corners before turning the pockets.

BOX CONSTRUCTION

- Cut required templates carefully. Accuracy is essential.
- Cut or tear strips of fabric as specified.
- Fold side pocket strips in half, right sides together, and press.
- Lay out templates carefully across the strip with a 3 mm (⅛ inch) gap between each one and 1.5 mm at each end. Mark the seam line at each end.
- Sew the side seams, trim the side seam allowance to 9 mm (⅜ inch) and trim across the top corners, turn inside out and press.
- Re-position the templates along the folded edge of the pocket. Note that the spaces between each template should be even and the templates placed in the correct order if all the side panels are not identical in size.
- Draw a line between each template and mark the bottom of this line at the base of the template (fig. 5-1).
- Remove templates. Turn both raw edges in, in line with the bottom mark just made and pin, ready to sew down each vertical division between box sides (fig. 5-1). Note that one pin in line with each marked vertical line is sufficient.
- With matching thread and commencing at the bottom edge, sew up the marked line to the top fold. Stop the stitching at the fold with the needle in the down position. Turn the fabric and stitch down the seam covering the first stitching line. Note that double stitching in this way leaves all thread ends at the point where the boxes are sewn together and thus well hidden.

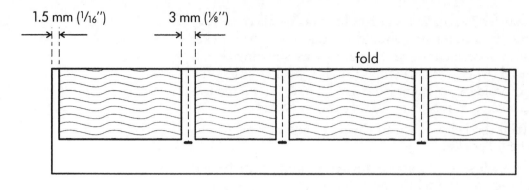

1.5 mm (¹⁄₁₆″)   3 mm (⅛″)   fold

(not to scale)

Fig 5-1

- All templates are covered with Pellon; usually one layer for the outside of the box and two for the inside. This must be sewn in place around the templates to prevent slipping when inserting them into the pockets. Stretch the wadding firmly around the templates, cutting it flush with the edges. Stitch the Pellon together working over the edges of the plastic. Do not allow the Pellon to bunch outside the edges of the templates. Extra layers of padding can be added if desired, but remember this may require extra fabric allowance for each pocket.

- Push covered templates into the fabric pockets. To make this process easier, the plastic can be rolled gently then flattened out inside the pocket, thus enabling irregular shapes to be inserted through small openings. Make sure all seam allowances are smoothed out and laying to the inside of the box.

- Tuck the bottom edges of the templates behind the seam allowances on the outside of the panel.

- Slip stitch the pockets closed. This seam should be on the inside when the box is constructed.

- Make a single pocket for the box base and complete in the same way.

- Cut a lining for the box top and match the right sides together. Stitch together along the stitching line already marked, leaving one side (preferably the back edge) open for turning. For a neater finish on all corners, carry the machine stitching round the back corners as shown on the diagram. Trim the fabric across the corners, turn and insert the template by rolling it to fit through the opening. Slip stitch the opening closed.

- Match the two ends of the side strip together and ladder stitch firmly together using strong thread (Coton Perle No. 8 or linen thread are excellent).

- Fit the sides to the base and ladder stitch in place. Note: place the seamed edge next to the base with the handsewn corner to the back of the box.

- Finish the lid and any tray inserts in the same way. Leave a small gap in the stitching at the centre back of the lid to allow for decorative cord ends to be tucked in.

- Sew a decorative cord around the box top to hide the seam or work around the top with a row of palestrina knot stitch using a heavy thread.

Note that the lid of the box may be finished without side panels and hinged to the box by ladder stitching across the back edge. A button and loop can be used to hold the box closed.

BASIC RECTANGULAR BOX

Finished size: 15 cm x 10 cm x 7 cm deep (6 " x 4" x 3")

Requirements

30 cm (12") homespun or calico fabric

50 cm Pellon or soft sew Vilene

45 cm x 31 cm (18" x 12") sheet of template plastic
    For embroidery requirements and details refer to page 44.

- Cut templates as detailed in fig. 5-2a & 5-2b.

- Cut fabric as follows:
    2 pieces 18 cm x 12 cm (7" x 5") for lid
    1 piece 20 cm x 17 cm (8" x 7") for base
    1 piece 16 cm x 50 cm (6½" x 20") for sides
    1 piece   9 cm x 50 cm (3½" x 20") for lid sides

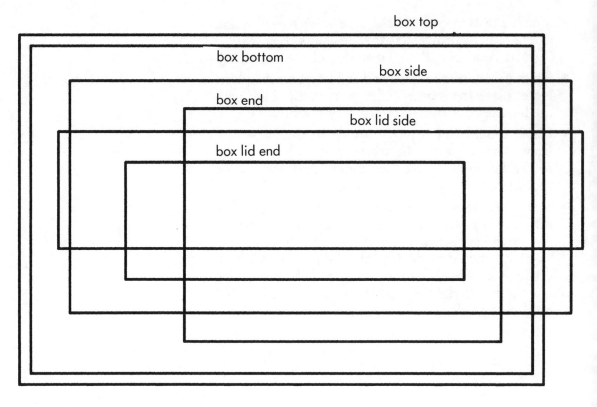

Fig 5-2a

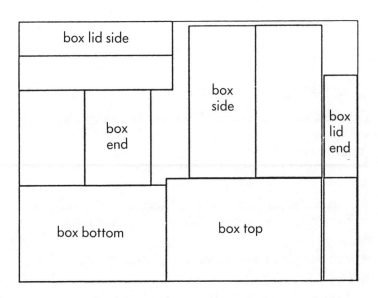

Fig 5-2b

HEXAGONAL BOX WITH TWO TRAYS

Finished size: 16 cm across x 7 cm deep (6½″ x 3″)
Requirements — including trays
72 cm x 36 cm (29″ x 15″) plain fabric for lid, base
and tray bases
112 cm x 25 cm (45″ x 10″) patterned fabric for all
sides of box and trays
50 cm Pellon or soft sew Vilene
45 cm x 31 cm (18″ x 12″) sheet of template plastic

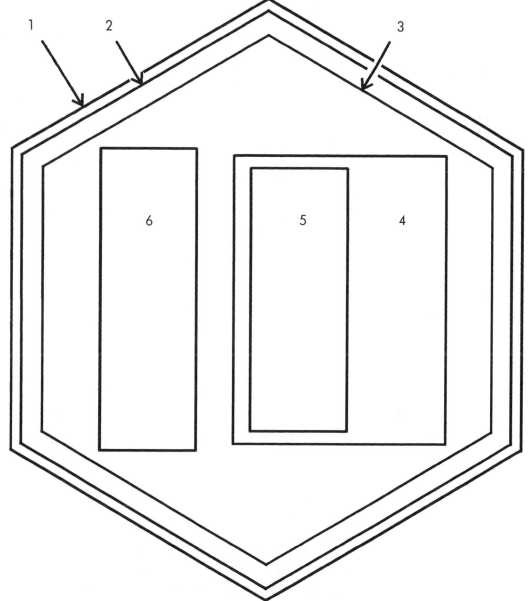

1. box lid top 2. box base 3. inner tray base
4. box side 5. inner tray sides 6. box lid side

Full-size templates

Fig 5-3a

For embroidery requirements and details refer to page 42.

- Cut templates as detailed in fig. 5-3a and 5-3b.
- Cut fabric as follows:

  Plain fabric
  8 pieces 18 cm (7″) square for the lid and all bases
  Patterned fabric
  1 piece 54 cm x 14 cm (21½″ x 5½″) for the box sides
  3 pieces 54 cm x 8 cm (21½″ x 3″) for the lid and tray sides

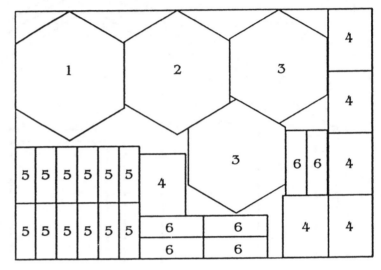

Fig 5-3b   1. box lid top 2. box base 3. inner tray base
4. box sides 5. inner tray sides 6. box lid sides

ELONGATED OCTAGONAL BOX WITH TRAY INSERTS

Finished size: 22 cm x 12 cm x 9 cm deep (9″ x 5″ x 3½″)
Requirements — including one full tray + one 3-piece tray
112 cm x 45 cm (45″ x 18″) plain fabric for outside of box and tray bases
112 cm x 40 cm (45″ x 16″) patterned fabric for inside of box and sides of trays
1 metre (36″) Pellon or soft sew Vilene
77 cm x 30 cm (30″ x 12″) template plastic
For embroidery requirements and details refer to page 40.

- Cut templates as detailed in fig. 5-4a and 5-4b.

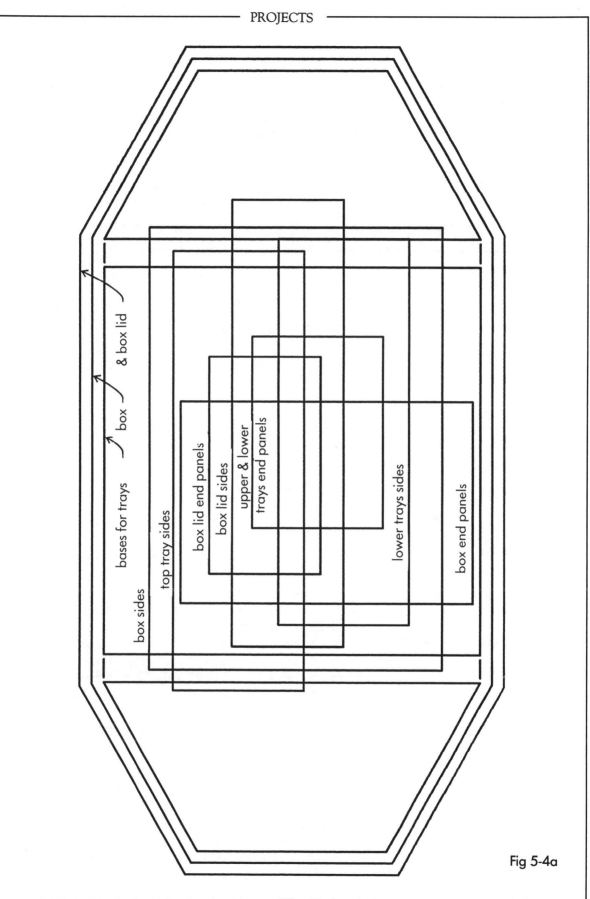

bases for trays

& box lid

box

box sides

top tray sides

box lid end panels

box lid sides

upper & lower
trays end panels

lower trays sides

box end panels

Fig 5-4a

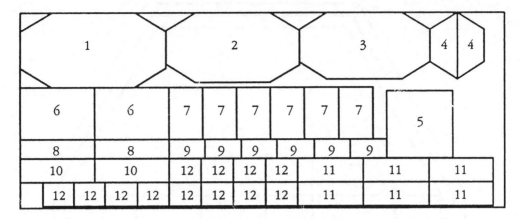

Layout on plastic sheet 770 mm x 300 mm

1. box lid top. 2. box base 3. top tray base
4. lower end tray base. 5. lower middle tray base
6. box side. 7. box end panel
8. box lid side. 9. box lid end panel
10. top tray side. 11. lower trays side
12. upper & lower trays end panel

Fig 5-4b

- Cut fabric as follows:
  Plain fabric:
  one 63 cm x 11 cm (25″ x 4½″) box sides (outside)
  one 63 cm x 9 cm (25″ x 3½″) lid sides
  five 25 cm x 15cm (10″ x 6″) top, base and tray bases
  one 26 cm x 13 cm (10½″ x 5″) tray base
  two 13 cm x 12 cmm (5″ x 5″) tray base
  Patterned fabric:
  one 63 cm x 11 cm (25″ x 4½″) box sides (lining)
  one 25 cm x 15 cm (10″ x 6″) top lining
  one 60 cm x 11 cm (24″ x 4½″) tray sides
  one 40 cm x 10 cm (16″ x 4″) centre bottom tray sides
  two 30 cm x 10 cm (12″ x 4″) end tray sides

Special Construction Notes;

- Place the two box side pieces right sides together and mark a seam line 16 mm (⅜″) from the top edge.
- Position templates along this line to establish side seam positions. Stitch along the side seams and the top of the pocket before continuing as before.

NEEDLE BOX

This needle box is constructed in the same way as the boxes described earlier. Pockets are used along the folding section to hold packets of needles or cards of thread etc. Refer to the instructions for the basic box for more detail.

Requirements
Outer fabric 115 cm x 30 cm (45" x 12")
Contrast pockets fabric 62 cm x 13 cm (24½" x 5")
30 cm (12") Pellon or soft sew Vilene
42.5 cm x 25 cm (17" x 10") template plastic
Embroidery threads:
Coton Perle No. 8 in toning colour and green
DMC Flower thread in cream or selected colour
Gold beads and charms as desired.

- Cut out templates as detailed in fig. 5-5a and 5-5b.
- Cut fabric as follows:
  Main colour
  one 62 cm x 26 cm (24½" x 10½")
  one 38 cm x 24 cm (15" x 9½")
  one 14 cm x 14 cm (5½" x 5½")
  Contrast colour
  one 62 cm x 13 cm (24½" x 5")

Special Construction Notes:
Contrast Pocket Strip

- Fold the fabric in half and sew the long edges together allowing a 5 mm (¼ inch) seam allowance.

- Press seam open, turn right side out and press, centring the seam down the centre back of the piece.

- Place the pocket section along the 62 cm length of the fabric, 2 cm up from the bottom of the strip. Sew in place across the bottom edge.

- Fold the strip in half, right sides together and press. Lay the templates along the strip, carefully dividing it as shown in fig. 5-5c. Note that the gaps between the templates have been carefully calculated to allow the strip to fold correctly when finished.

- Continue construction as detailed for the basic box side panel.

Outer Box

- Transfer the design to the lower right-hand corner of the 38 cm x 24 cm fabric strip.

- Construct box as detailed for the basic box.

Fig 5-5a

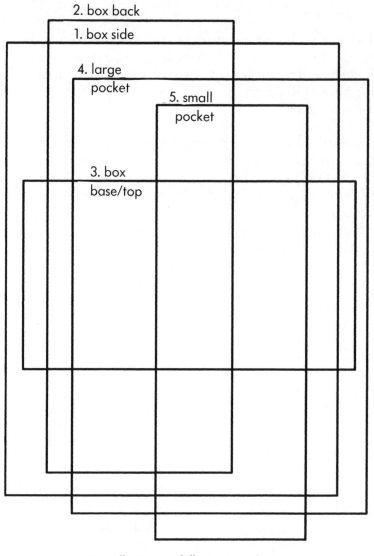

2. box back
1. box side
4. large pocket
5. small pocket
3. box base/top

Needle Box — full size template

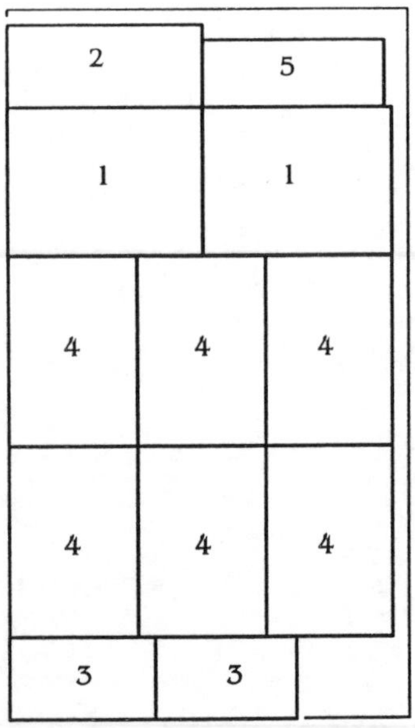

Fig 5-5b

1. box side 4. large pocket
2. box back 5. small pocket
3. box base/top

Needle Box layout
sheet size 250 mm x 425 mm (10" x 17")

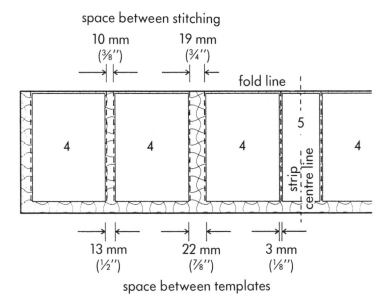

space between stitching

10 mm
(3/8")

19 mm
(3/4")

fold line

5

strip
centre line

4   4   4   4

13 mm
(1/2")

22 mm
(7/8")

3 mm
(1/8")

space between templates

Fig 5-5c

COSY CARRY

This garment makes a wonderful gift for an elderly or handicapped person. It is easy to wear, the shawl style top keeps the shoulders warm and the deep pockets are useful to carry small items such as a purse, a small piece of handwork or even a paperback book. It is ideal for those with limited mobility and those who find it difficult to carry small items. For extra security a zip can be inserted across the top of the pockets.

Make it up in tartan or plain fabric and it would be equally acceptable for a man.

Any fabric can be used, the version shown is made in polar fleece, a lovely soft cotton knit fabric with a brushed finish on both sides. Wool blanketing, or any other woollen fabric, can be used for extra warmth. A summer version can be made in lightweight cotton fabrics.

Requirements

Pattern for a straight cardigan-style jacket or vest with a dropped shoulder, in the size required, or make a pattern as shown in the diagram fig. 5-6.

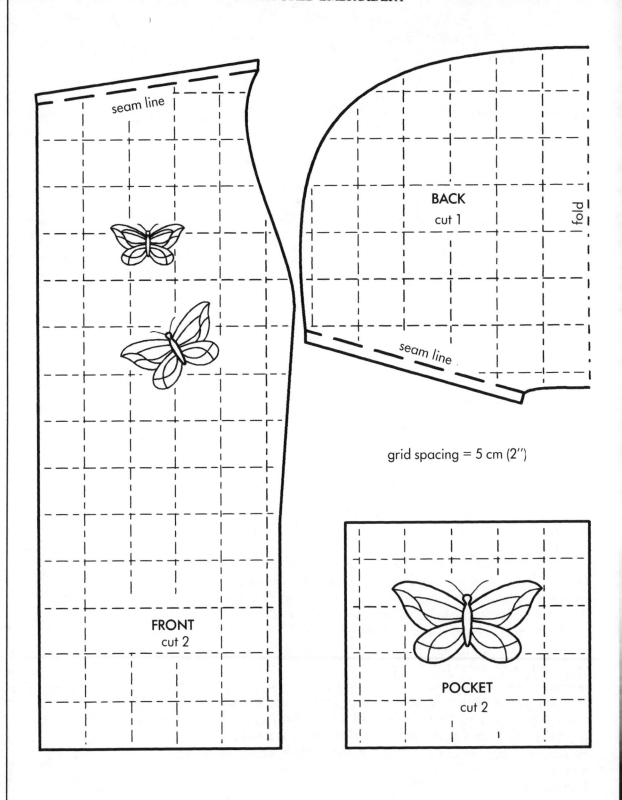

seam line

BACK
cut 1

fold

seam line

grid spacing = 5 cm (2″)

FRONT
cut 2

POCKET
cut 2

Fig 5-6

Cosy Carry ¼ full size

Approximately 1 metre of 150 cm wide (40″ x 60″ wide) — dependent on finished length required.

Fold over braid to encase all edges.

Thin Vilene to back embroidered area if working on stretch fabric.

- Prepare pattern from fig. 5-6 or modify bought pattern accordingly.

- Transfer the design as described on page 6.

- Work the chosen embroidery design on the pockets and shoulder line, backing the area with Vilene if working on stretch fabric.

- Join shoulder seams.

- Bind the top edge of the pocket piece.

- With right sides together, sew the pocket to the lower front edge. Fold the pocket up along the seam line and pin the raw edges together.

- Encase all raw edges in fold over braid or a bias binding.

SCISSOR HOLDER

The holder pictured is decorated with knotted lace worked from the book *Knotted Lace* by Elena Dickson and published by Sally Milner Publishing. However, purchased lace edging and beading will look just as pretty if you do not have the time or inclination to make your own lace.

Requirements
35 cm x 15 cm (14″ x 6″) homespun or similar fabric
35 cm x 15 cm (14″ x 6″) Pellon or soft sew Vilene
1 metre of 20 mm wide (40″ x ¾″) ribbon
2 metres (80″) entredeaux
1 metre beading for ribbon insertion
1 metre ribbon for insertion
3 metres lace edging for insertion and scissor holder
2 metal rings   one 45 mm (1¾″) inside diameter
                one 25 mm (1″) inside diameter
15 cm x 15 cm (6″ x 6″) template plastic

- Cut plastic templates from the pattern.

- Using the method given on page 6, mark the design from fig. 5-7a, including the outline for the front of the scissor case, on to the homespun backed with the Pellon.

- Work the embroidery using Coton Perle No. 12 and palestrina stitch for the line work. The roses are worked in Leah's No. 12 variegated Coton Perle (DMC Flower thread is a good alternative).

- From fig. 5-7b, trace the outline of the template for the back of the case onto the wrong side of the homespun.

- Back the front and back marked pieces with a second piece of fabric, right sides together, and sew around the edges. Stitch 1 mm ($\frac{1}{25}''$) outside the marked lines but leave open between A and B for turning and insertion of the templates.

- Cut out both pieces. Trim the Pellon back to the seam line on the front section and turn right side out.

- Cover the templates with Pellon as described for the box construction on page 66.

- Slide the templates into the pockets and hem stitch the opening closed.

- Slip stitch lace along the top edge of the front pocket.

- Place the two pieces together and ladder stitch with strong thread. Slip stitch lace in place around the outer edge.

To make the strap

- Join the entredeaux down both edges of the beading and join lace edging to the other side of the entredeaux.

- Thread ribbon through the beading and back the strip with the wide ribbon, sewing down the centre of the entredeaux on both sides to join.

- Attach one end to the back of the scissor holder.

To make the thread holder

- Bind the two rings with Coton Perle No. 5 or 8 working buttonhole stitch over the ring. Pack the stitches very close to completely cover the metal and turn the ridged edge of the stitching to the inside of the ring.

- Fill in the small ring, working a crisscross of stitches across the ring and passing the needle through the ridged edge of the binding to hold them firmly in place. Pad the centre with a circle of Pellon or a small amount of wadding as you work.

- Gather a piece of narrow lace to fit around the edge

of the smaller ring and sew in place.

- Work a posy of roses, starting in the centre of the ring and adding some green leaves between the flowers.

- With strong thread stitch the two rings together at the top and sew the other end of the strap to the back of the rings.

The scissor case illustrated is also decorated with a collection of tiny scissor charms on the holder and along the strap.

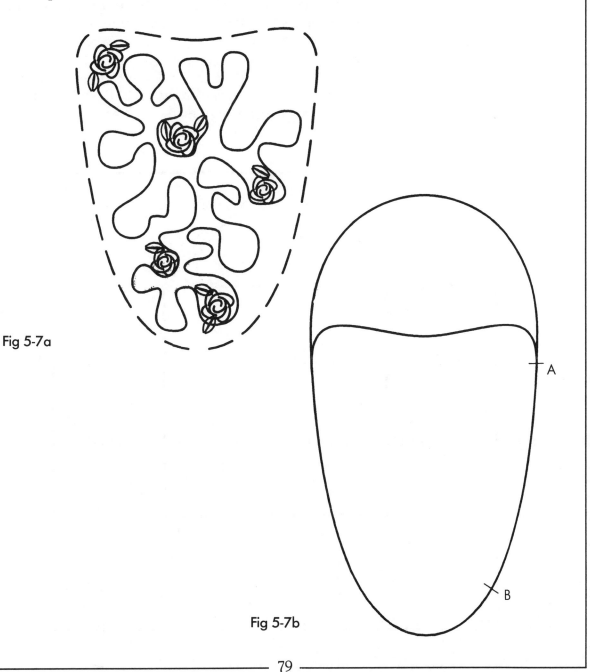

Fig 5-7a

Fig 5-7b

PIN CUSHION

This is a simple little pin cushion worked on canvas, using a mixture of continental or tent stitch, colonial knots and Parisian stitch on the back.

The work will be more even if a small frame is used.

Requirements

18 cm square (7″) of canvas (20 or 22 threads per inch)

Variegated thread 'Watercolours' by Caron used for the centre (colour no. 59). Paternayan yarn can be substituted.

Paternayan yarn colour no. 716, 845 and A604 are used for colonial knots and A604 is also used for the outer triangles.

- Mark a square 12 cm x 12 cm (4¾″) in the centre of the canvas. Find the mid-point of each side and mark a second square as shown in fig. 5-8. Find the mid-point again and mark a third square in the middle.

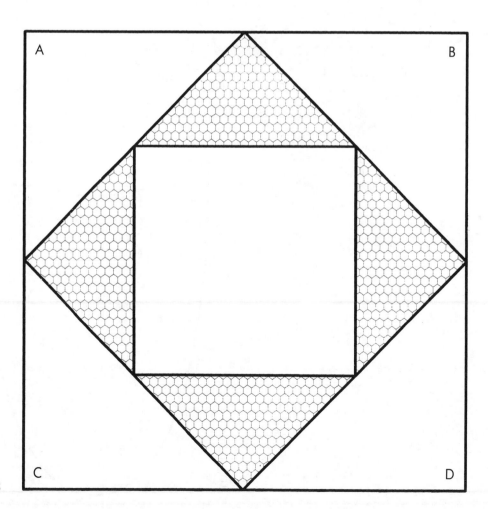

Fig 5-8

- Fill the centre square with continental or tent stitch using a single strand of variegated thread or Paternayan yarn.
- Fill in the marked area with colonial knots. Pack them very tightly, working with one strand and using a variety of the Paternayan threads.
- Fill in the remaining areas with Parisian or tent stitch in a single strand of Paternayan Yarn.
- Trim canvas, leaving a 5 mm (¼″) seam allowance. Finger press the seam allowance to the wrong side.
- Bring points A, B, C and D together at the centre back with the right sides facing out.
- Oversew the edges together along the folded turnings.
- Stuff before completely closing the final seam.

JEWELLERY

Specialty needlework shops usually stock a range of mounts suitable for jewellery pieces. Mounts originally designed to display photographs can often be found in antique shops and can be used for a very special piece (fig. 5-9).

- For ease of mounting embroidery in this type of frame, use fine fabric and stiffen it with iron-on Vilene.
- Mark the outline of the finished piece on the Vilene. Embroider the design, positioning it carefully within the marked outline, Cut out the stiffened disc and insert it into the frame in place of the photograph.

Less expensive jewellery can be made using porcelain china painting discs for a base. (fig. 5-10).

Fig 5-9

Fig 5-10a

Fig 5-10b

- Using fine fabric, work the design and cut it out, allowing sufficient fabric around the edge to run a strong gathering thread.
- Pull up firmly around the china disc and fasten securely.
- Cut a backing piece from felt or suede and sew in place.
- Sew on a brooch pin for fastening.

Interesting brooches can be made using metal rings in various sizes.

- Each ring is bound with thread working buttonhole stitch over the ring, packing the stitches as closely as possible.
- Turn the corded edge of the binding to the appropriate side of the ring so that the woven threads can be attached through these stitches.
- Weave a base of threads across the area to be filled with embroidery and place a piece of felt or Pellon between these threads to give a firm area to work on.

HAT BROOCH

Worked on a single ring 3 cm (1¼″) diameter.

- Prepare as detailed above. Add extra padding to create a slightly domed base to work on.
- Gather a piece of narrow lace and sew around the outer edge of the padding.
- Fill the centre with colonial knots in a fine wool, using 2 or 3 shaded colours plus green.
- Add a tiny bow in 2 mm silk ribbon over the join in the lace.
- Back with a circle of felt if desired.
- Sew on a brooch pin.

DOUBLE RING BROOCHES

These brooches can be used to hold a pair of spectacles or as a thread holder (see Scissor Holder).

Rings of various sizes can be used. The brooch pictured and shown in fig. 5-11 is made from one ring of 35 mm (1⅜″) diameter and one ring of 15 mm (⅝″) diameter.

Fig 5-11

- Place the bound rings together and stitch firmly where they touch.
- Cover the remaining area with woven threads and fill this area with embroidery as shown.
- Sew a small brooch pin behind the embroidery.

COAT HANGER COVERS

These soft padded hangers are easy to make and the covers can be removed for laundering.

Requirements
46 cm x 26 cm (18" x 10") blanketing
45 cm x 35 cm (18" x 14") firm wadding and small amount of toy stuffing
15 cm (6") bias binding to cover the hook
50 cm (20") ribbon for decoration
2 metres (2 yards) x 5 cm (2") wide lace edging
1 wooden coat hanger

- Cut two strips of wadding 45 cm x 8 cm (18" x 3") and wind firmly around each end of the hanger.
- Cut out the wadding according to the pattern (fig. 5-12).
- Sew darts and side seams, turn right side out and fit over the hanger (hook removed).
- Add toy stuffing to pad area under the hanger and machine sew the lower edge closed using a zigzag stitch.
- Cover the hook with satin bias binding. Re-press the binding with one raw edge across until it almost touches the other folded edge and press. Fold in half again and stitch carefully with a zigzag stitch very close to the edge, folding in one end as you stitch. Slip over the hook, pull down tightly and trim to expose the screw end.
- Replace hook and sew base of covering firmly to the wadding.
- Cut outer cover from blanketing and embroider with chosen design.
- Sew darts and side seams.
- Gather lace and zigzag around the bottom edge.
- Pierce a hole for the hook, neaten with buttonhole stitch or seal with a washable fabric glue.
- Slip cover over the hanger and tie decorative bow around the hook to finish.

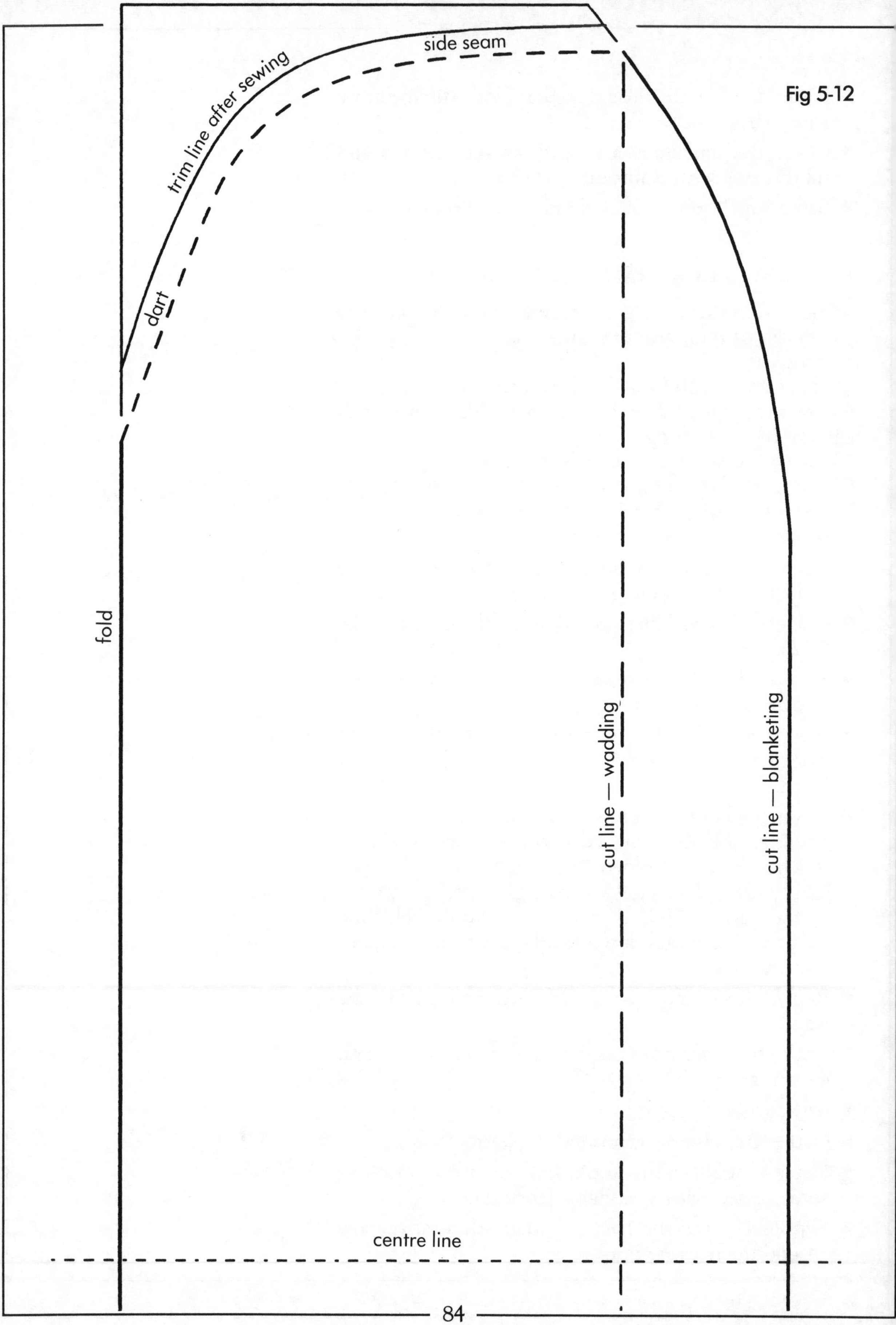

Fig 5-12

trim line after sewing

side seam

dart

fold

cut line — wadding

cut line — blanketing

centre line

84

CREAM ON CREAM SWEATER BY HELEN JANOCHA

Helen has designed and worked this beautiful sweater from Onkaparinga blanketing as a practical alternative to wool embroidery on blankets for her embroidery classes.

Requirements
Pattern for stretch knit sweater
Ivory, or winter white wool blanketing, according to pattern requirements. 170 cm x 160 cm wide (67" x 63") is sufficient for the sample shown in size 14 to 16 (with some wastage).
50 cm ribbing for sweater
  For details of embroidery and embroidery requirements, refer to page 54.
  Finish construction of the sweater according to the pattern instructions.

PUNCHNEEDLE EMBROIDERY

This form of embroidery originated in Russia and was used to embellish their beautiful traditional costumes. Worked with a special needle, the technique creates a beautiful texture of plush raised pile using embroidery threads.
  A variety of needles are available on the market and come with instructions for their use. Prices vary considerably, as does the basic design of the needles. They are available in various sizes suitable for use with a variety of different threads. A firmly woven fabric is easiest to work on. Further information on this subject can be found in *Russian Punchneedle Embroidery* by Gail Bird and published by Dover Publications, Inc., New York.

TEDDY BEAR BY PAT KANE

Requirements
10 cm (4") plastic hoop with a rim (e.g. Susan Bates brand)
DMC stranded cotton no. 435 (2 skeins), 433, 432
Black 2 black beads 4 mm (⅛") diameter
Scrap of 6 mm (¼") ribbon

- Trace the design (fig. 5-13) onto the wrong side of the fabric.
- Stretch fabric drum tight into the hoop.

Fig 5-13

- Set large needle gauge at 14 mm, thread with 6 strands of DMC 422 and punch in ears, face, hands and feet.
- Remove the fabric from the hoop and shear the work to form a velvet finish.
- Replace the fabric into the hoop, making sure it is drum tight once again.
- Outline the bear with 2 strands of DMC 433 in the medium-size needle set at 12 mm.
- Fill in bear with 3 strands of DMC 435 in the medium-size needle set at 12 mm.
- Work the nose in black satin stitch and the mouth in black back stitch.
- Sew on beads for the eyes and a ribbon bow tie.

BUSH SCENE NEEDLE PAINTING BY JOYCE MCKEE

(Picture Size 150 mm x 215 mm [6" x 8½"])

This is a beautiful form of textured embroidery that is not as difficult as it looks, if it is taken step by step.

- The picture is worked on calico, which must be very firmly stretched onto a frame approximately 28 cm x 36 cm (11" x 14"). Refer to fig. 5-14a.

- Gaberdine, or similar material, is used for the main background fabric. This fabric is particularly suitable as it does not snag or catch as heavier threads are worked through it. The colour is chosen to match the picture background, in this case, blue to match the sky. (The colour used in the original is similar to DMC stranded cotton colour number 813.)
- Transfer the outline of F1 (fig. 5-14b) to the gaberdine before tacking the gaberdine to the calico.
- Extra depth is given to the shading of the sky by tacking layers of blue silk organza (S1 and S2) firmly in place over the background (fig. 5-14a).

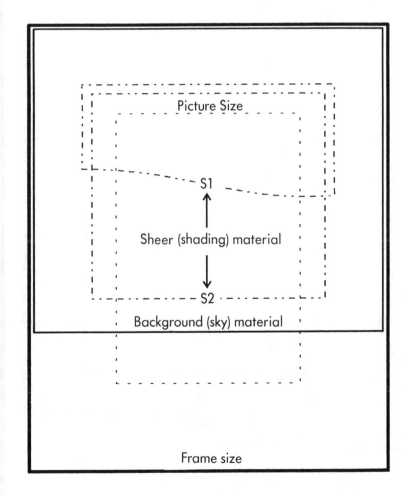

Fig 5-14a

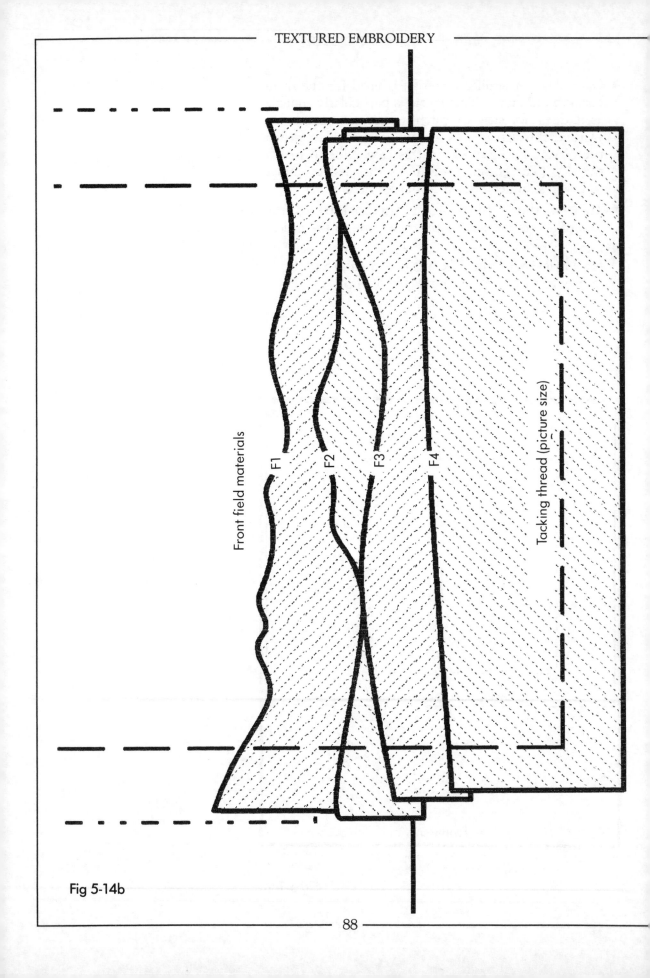

Front field materials

F1 F2 F3 F4

Tacking thread (picture size)

Fig 5-14b

- If clouds are required these are achieved by using wool fleece in white or grey. These are held in place by overlaying the whole area with a transparent chiffon or silk organza. Note that the overlay must be stretched firmly as it is tacked into place to prevent wrinkling once the embroidery has been started. This step is not easy to do and does require care and patience. It can be omitted without detriment to the finished piece as clear, intense blue skies are common in the Australian bush.

- Careful choice of fabrics is necessary for the foreground. I find the best range of plain cotton fabrics is available from a patchwork shop. To give a guide to the fabric colours used in the original picture, a DMC stranded cotton colour reference is as follows: F1 : 931, F2 : 3011, F3 : 437 and F4 : 436.

- Back the fabric with lightweight iron-on vilene, to prevent fraying, before cutting the shapes detailed in fig. 5-14b.

- Starting with the mountain section, F1, and matching it with the outline marked on the gaberdine, tack each piece in turn to the background finishing with the foreground F4.

- Mark the border of the picture with a tacking thread.

- The tree position must now be determined. This is done in one of two ways depending on how you choose to work the tree.

  (1) For the original picture, Joyce worked the main trunk and the largest branches of the tree that are not covered by any leaves, separately. These were worked using a round embroidery frame and with organdie as the base fabric (fig. 5-14c; shaded area only), then cut out and sewed to the background by turning a fine hem and stem stitching in place, using the same thread as used in the embroidery of the trunk. The raised stem band used for this process is not padded in any way when following this method and the raised texture results from packing the stitches very closely. Some might find the process of attaching the tree rather tedious, but working by this method means that one of the more time-consuming parts of the picture is more portable and can be carried around and worked on whenever convenient. If working the tree in this

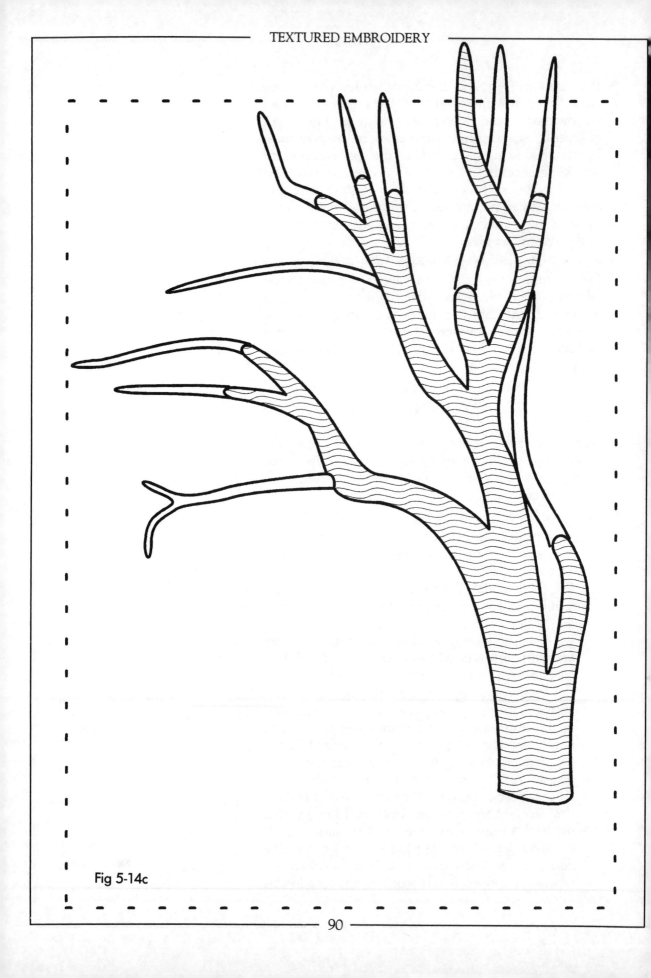

Fig 5-14c

way, mark the outline of the tree (fig. 5-14c) with tacking thread onto the background.

(2) My husband, Don, devised what may prove to be a simpler way of working the tree, which may be preferred by the less-experienced embroiderer. Copy the outline of the main trunk and branches (the shaded area only of fig. 5-14c) onto a piece of white felt. Cut out carefully and position onto the picture background. Tack in place. Where more padding is desired strands of wool can be added at this time under the felt as it is tacked in place. Work the horizontal stitches for the raised stem band across the felt, anchoring it firmly to the base fabric (fig. 2-21).

- Start by embroidering the blue mountains. Work French knots in the following colours:
  Appletons Crewel wool no. 323, 324, 325 and 201. Leave some spaces, allowing the fabric to give textured effect.

- For the foreground mountains, work French knots and seed stitch using Appletons Crewel wool colour no. 336 and 338.

- Work the tree using preferred method. Trunk and main branches in raised stem band using DMC stranded cotton in colours no. 347, 644, 645, 648, 822, 844, 3776 and Ecru. Use one strand for the horizontal or cross stitches and two strands for the stem stitches.

- If the tree is applied by method (1) above
  — after working the tree on the organdie, cut out (leaving about a 3 mm (⅛″) hem allowance), fold the hem allowance under and apply to the picture using stem stitch (do not stretch the trunk too tightly)
  — cover any organdie not turned in at the end of the branches.

- Smaller branches are added using stem stitch directly onto the background fabric. Join them by overlapping the stitching with the previously worked part of the tree.

- Leaves can now be added. Marking of the main leaf areas may help. The stitches used are: fly stitch (hanging upside down), straight stitch and lazy daisy stitch. The combination of stitching helps to give variety. Form leaf clusters making sure they always join onto the tree. Small branches may be added where appropriate. Work with a single strand of stranded cotton. Suitable DMC colours are: 934, 936, 469 and 581. Shaded colours such as Caron Waterlilies Olive and Leah's Over-dyed no. 57 are also excellent and were used selectively in the original. In general, the darker colour leaves are placed first and the lighter colour leaves superimposed over them.

- The final area worked is the foreground.
  Trees in French knots using
  Au Ver a Soie 3726 (or DMC stranded cotton 935), Caron Waterlilies Olive (or DMC stranded cotton 3052) and Needle Necessities over-dyed floss 142 (or DMC stranded cotton 3053 or 3364).
  Grasses in straight stitch placed to give grass look, as shown in the diagram, using threads such as: Needle Necessities 142 and over-dyed wool no. 62 (cream/gold) and Waterlilies Olive.
  Clutter — bark, rocks etc — in straight stitch using A Ver a Soie 524 and 2242
  Needle Necessities 161 or Leah's 110.
  Stem stitch log in DMC Medici 8500.
  Be careful to work around the tree base to make it blend into the foreground.

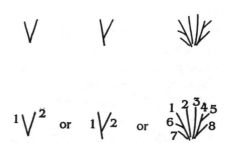

Other books by Jenny Bradford in the Milner Craft Series

Silk Ribbon Embroidery For Gifts and Garments
Bullion Stitch Embroidery From Roses to Wildflowers
Original Designs for Silk Ribbon Embroidery
Original Designs for Smocking

Any queries for the author should be directed to:
Jenny Bradford
PO Box 5
Scullin ACT 2614
Australia
Phone and fax: (06) 254 6814